Jobs and the Military Spouse

Jobs *and the* Military Spouse

Second Edition

Janet Farley

IMPACT PUBLICATIONS
Manassas Park, Virginia

Jobs and the Military Spouse

ISBN: 1-57023-201-6

Library of Congress: 2003100525

Publisher: For information on Impact Publications, including current and forthcoming publications, authors, press kits, online bookstore, and submission requirements, visit our website: www.impactpublications.com

Publicity/Rights: For information on publicity, author interviews, and subsidary rights, contact the Media Relations Department: Tel. 703-361-7300, Fax 703-335-9486, or email: info@impactpublications.com.

Sales/Distribution: All bookstore sales are handled through Impact's trade distributor: National Book Network, 15200 NBN Way, Blue Ridge Summit, PA 17214, Tel. 1-800-462-6420. All other sales and distribution inquiries should be directed to the publisher: Sales Department, IMPACT PUBLICATIONS, 9104 Manassas Drive, Suite N, Manassas Park, VA 20111-5211, Tel. 703-361-7300, Fax 703-335-9486, or email: info@impactpublications.com.

Contents

Preface ix

1. It's Not Just a Job 1
   - Life in the Mobile Employment Lane   2
   - Developing Job Search Focus   4
   - Taking Control   6

2. Begin At the Beginning 7
   - What Do You Have to Offer?   8
   - Compile Your Career History   8
   - Identify Your Skills   13
   - Updating Your Skills   18
   - The Money Issue   18
   - Identifying Your Job Objective   19
   - Knowing What Employers Want   22
   - Finding a Fit That Works for You   25

3. Planning for Success 26
   - The Tale of Two Spouses   27
   - Why You Need a Plan   27
   - The Full Circle Job Search Plan   28
   - Establishing Realistic Goals   34
   - Keeping Track of What You Do   34
   - Managing Your Time   37
   - Avoiding the Job Search Blues   37
   - Achieving Success   38

4. Options That Work 39
   - Federal Employment – Appropriated Funds   40
   - Non-Appropriated Fund Positions   43
   - Defense Contracting   44
   - Military Exchange System   45
   - Self-Employment   45
   - Private Industry   47
   - Opportunities Abroad   48

- Volunteering 48
- Using Your Imagination 49

5. Job Search Power Tools 50
- Networking: Is Your Net Working? 51
- Your References 53
- Your Communication Skills 56
- Face-to-Face 56
- Over the Telephone 57
- Online Communication 58
- Your Traditional Job Search Skills 60
- Employment Applications 65
- Your Mindset 69
- Your Follow-Up 69

6. Creating an Outstanding Resume 70
- Why You Need a Resume 70
- The Truth About Employers 71
- Creating Your Masterpiece 71
- Language and Key Words 79
- The Adaptable Resume 82

7. Job Search Letters That Mean Business 93
- The Cover Letter 94
- The Lost Art of Writing Thank You Letters 100
- Letter Resumes 103
- Job Search Letter and Email Strategies 105

8. Interviewing With Ease 106
- Getting to Know You 106
- Interview Purposes and Types 107
- Potentially Illegal & Discriminatory Questions 115
- Questions to Ask Employers 117
- Your Interview Ensemble 118
- The Interview 119
- What to Do After an Interview 120
- Make It a Two-Way Street 121

9. Negotiating and Evaluating Job Offers 122
- Evaluating the Job Offer 123
- Negotiating Basics 125
- Salary History 129

Contents

- Benefits 130
- Work Schedules, Locations and Contents 131
- When You Don't Get Offered a Job 133
- Becoming Fit 133

10. Managing Your Own Career 134
- On Your Own 134
- Creating Your Own Advancement 135
- When You Decide to Leave a Job 138
- When You Decide to Leave the Military Lifestyle 139
- Having a Successful Career 141
- Married, Mobile, and Motivated 142

Red, White, and Blue Family Centers 145

Red, White, and Blue Pages 147

Index 151

The Author 155

Career Resources 157

Preface

BEING A MILITARY SPOUSE has never been a job for the thin-skinned or faint of heart. It is a grueling, sometimes thankless job, as world events such as September 11, 2001 so brutally reminded us. After the tragedy, the role of the military spouse had only just begun. In addition to grieving with the nation, we had to shoulder the burden that our spouses, while always ready for war, had been called actively into harm's way once again. And through it all, life just goes on whether our spouses are off fighting in a war a world away or doing their part at home. If military spouses can be stereotyped, then I'd put my money on the word *resilient*. Thankfully, it is that very characteristic which will make your job search, and anything you strive to achieve in life, a successful endeavor.

Military spouses, as you well know, are a unique and diverse population. She could be the young woman, fresh out of high school or college, who has married a special ops sergeant or a new 2nd Lt. He could be the 38 year old network analyst or the 45 year old infantry sergeant major who just retired from the military and whose wives are still on active duty. Perhaps she is the 27 year old nurse, with two kids who must work to help make ends meet. Or maybe she is a dedicated community volunteer, in her late 50's and married to a general. Anyone can be a military spouse and that's what makes it all so interesting.

Since its initial publication in 1997, *Jobs and the Military Spouse* has assisted thousands of family members in seeking and finding fulfilling employment, wherever they have been stationed. It is a book which was written from the heart and mind of a fellow spouse who has known all too well how incredibly challenging it can be to be married to someone in uniform and still try to maintain professional continuity of her own.

The aim of this revised edition is to make your job search easier for you. If you can find fulfillment as an employed individual, then everyone wins. You're satisfied. Your family is happy and the military benefits as well. Let's not forget that corporate America also benefits. Companies such as the Marriott™, CVS, Home Depot· and Adecco have led the way in actively tapping into the talented and skilled workforce that is found within the military spouse population. In summary, it's a good thing all around.

In this revised edition, you'll find that over half the book has been updated to provide you with the best possible information necessary to guide you in your job search. The Red, White and Blue Pages have also been updated to include invaluable online resources for your use. I welcome suggestions and comments from you. Please feel free to email me at janetfarley@hotmail.com.

For their professional assistance and support, I'd like to thank Elizabeth Grant of the Heidelberg, Germany Army Community Services and Jean Marie Ward of the OSD. I'm also grateful to Susan Loden and Michele Susan Hitchcock of the Wuerzberg, Germany Army Community Service and to Farley for everything.

It is my sincere hope that *Jobs and the Military Spouse* is a resource that will help you achieve your career goals.

Good luck and happy hunting!

Janet I. Farley, Ed.M.

Jobs and the Military Spouse

1

It's Not Just a Job

THE UNFORGIVING MIDDAY SUN beats down on the lone figure sweating his way though the barren desert. You are an army of one, the commercial suggests. Ironically, it is often the military spouse who feels alone and challenged as she (or he) tries to survive and thrive in an unforgiving job market while delicately balancing her goals and dreams with those of Uncle Sam. As any spouse will readily tell you, the two sides don't always compliment each other.

"I worked as a GS-6, general clerk, with career status in civil service before I got married. I thought my status would work to my benefit as we moved around from place to place, but I was wrong. Every time we've moved so far, I've had to accept a job one or two grade levels lower. It seems like I'm always starting over." – Sheila Ahner, military spouse

"It takes a lot of effort to find a new job with every move. It could even take up to a year to find one. Even then, some employers won't hire you if they know you're married to someone in the military. They know that in two to three years, or sooner, you'll leave again and they don't want to waste the money or the time training you. It's not easy being a male spouse, either. A lot of people think that if you're a military spouse, you are a woman. Sometimes it's as though you don't even exist." – Al Goodwin, military spouse

"At one duty station, I worked off post with a temporary agency as a staffing specialist. A week didn't go by that I didn't witness discrimination against military spouses by one of the other staffing specialists. I finally asked her why she wouldn't place qualified military spouses in those positions. She said that if she did that, she would only be making more work for herself in the long run. She also said that some employers specifically requested 'local' candidates for the same reason." – Irene Fain, military spouse

Being married to the military has its advantages and disadvantages. It can offer many wonderful opportunities. You might get to travel the world, meet people from different walks of life and have experiences others can only dream about in their lifetime. It's not always so wonderful, though, if you are trying to juggle a job or a career within this often nomadic, always changing, and frequently stressful lifestyle.

In a perfect world, you could have your job or advance your career and be happily married to someone in uniform. Life in the mobile employment lane, while somewhat improved, is still far from perfect.

Life in the Mobile Employment Lane

Once upon a time military spouses were known as "dependents." The majority of these dependents, generally women, would never dream of having a job, much less a professional career, outside the boundaries of their homes. Nevertheless, they did have a job description that was quite clear. They were expected to stay home, raise the children, and fully support their husband's career whether he was a buck private or a three-star general. The military did not always openly concern itself with the home life of its forces. After all, if they had wanted their troops married, they would have issued them wives in the first place. End of story, right?

Fortunately, that's not the end of the story at all. Today, spouses and family members make up 58.5% of the military family while active duty service members make up 41.5%. Ninety-three percent of spouses are female and nearly seven percent are male. Seventy percent of the 693,793 spouses are 35 years old or younger and enjoying their prime earning years in the workforce. Forty-eight percent of officers' spouses in the United States alone are employed and an additional seven percent of spouses are seeking work. In a 1997 Survey of Military Spouses conducted by the Defense Manpower Data Center, 55% of enlisted spouses were working and eight percent were looking for employment. As a result of such numbers and the effect they have on our active duty population, the Department of Defense has changed the way it thinks about family members and spouses throughout the years. It has come to realize the enormous impact that spouses have on the retention rate of its fighting forces, an issue dear to its heart. They discovered that happy soldiers, sailors, airmen, and marines tended to stay in the military. Those who were unhappy did not. They left the armed forces when their contracts ended, they took with them valuable technological skills, leaving the military to spend more dollars retraining others in their place. Even in periods of downsizing, such as we have witnessed in recent years, it is vital that the military maintain a certain level of readiness and competence. A 1999 Active Duty Survey (Defense Manpower Data Center) further revealed that service members married to spouses who were employed in civilian jobs or who were voluntarily in the workforce tended to be more satisfied with the military way of life than those of other married military personnel.

As a result of such survey findings, support programs such as the employment readiness programs found in the military family support and services and the transition assistance programs were created and have helped countless spouses (and military members) find fulfilling employment throughout the world. On a national level, such organizations as the National Military Family Association (NMFA) and the Department of Defense's (DoD) Office of Family Policy actively represent spouses and family members on a wide variety of issues, including employment.

Even with such great support, it is still challenging (to say the least) to be married to the military and employed at the same time. Frequent moves make it difficult to get your foot on the first step of the career ladder, much less up it. Constantly having to relocate can prevent you from building up seniority with a particular company, which in turn can prevent you from taking full advantage of certain benefits such as retirement pay and savings plans. Every time you move, you stop bringing in a paycheck, and this can take a toll on the standard of living enjoyed by your family. Underemployment is also a nemesis of the mobile lifestyle. You may have a master's degree in rocket science, but if no one is looking to hire a rocket scientist you may have to settle for something totally out of your field.

In addition to the findings above, spouses report that employers will often shy away from hiring anyone married to the military. They (the employers) assume that the spouse will not stay with their company for any length of time before moving on to another place.

Life in the mobile employment lane may not seem like a life at all, unless you approach it with the right attitude. Think of the obstacles you face as challenges rather than difficulties. You can make the best of your situation regardless of your circumstances. The choice is yours.

Developing Job Search Focus

One way to begin making the best of your situation is to develop job search **FOCUS**, a five-point strategy for conducting an effective job search campaign:

1. Formulate a "full circle" job search plan
2. Overcome any weaknesses by promoting your strengths
3. Choose to take responsibility for your own employment situation
4. Use and expand your existing network of resources
5. Succeed according to your own standards

Formulate a Full Circle Job Search Plan

When you try to find a job without a job search plan, a strategy for success, you short-change yourself. You open yourself up to a hit-or-miss approach to managing your own career. A full circle job search plan eliminates that potential blunder. With a full circle plan, your actions continue even after you find a job. Here are the steps in the circle:

- Decide upon or re-evaluate your career direction.
- Develop and implement a plan which supports that career direction. It should include specific goals and a game plan for obtaining them.
- Work to achieve those goals.

- Close the "circle" by deciding upon or re-evaluating your career direction on a periodic basis.

A full circle job search plan is really a career management tool that you control. Your plan doesn't have to be written in ink. Flexibility is required! Life is not stagnant. You change. Your career aspirations may also change and that's great. No problem. You can handle it with a full circle approach. Chapter 3, "Planning for Success," shows you how to develop a full circle job search plan and quickly put it into action.

Overcome Any Weaknesses By Promoting Your Strengths

Imagine that you are sitting in an interview right this very moment. A potential employer asks you if you have ever supervised any other employees. Technically, you may not have ever held the job title of supervisor. Realistically, you may have supervised others in a number of different situations. You could answer that question by saying that you do not have any supervisory experience. A better answer, however, would be to say that you have supervised others in a number of situations and give an example. By doing this, you concentrate more on selling what you do have (supervisory skills) rather than focusing on what you don't have (a specific job title in your past). Promoting your strengths also means enhancing them. You have to foster your own professional growth through any available means. Chapter 2 discusses this in more detail.

Take Responsibility For Your Own Employment Situation

"I am convinced that life is 10% of what happens to me and 90% how I react to it." – Charles Swindoll

Have you ever heard other spouses complain about how hard it was to get a job? Did they blame employers for their lack of success? Their current duty station? The military? Don't be discouraged or influenced by someone's testimony of "bad luck." The reality is that those spouses have chosen to push their responsibility off onto someone or something else. They haven't yet owned up to the fact that they are the ones who determine their success, or lack thereof, in the world at large. If you haven't already taken responsibility for your own situation, do so today. You'll feel much better about it in the long run and set an example for others to follow.

Use and Expand Your Existing Network of Resources

The military is a small world and it seems like it gets smaller every day. Chances are you know people all over the world. Networking with those people and meeting new people will serve you well in your job search. There's no other way to say it. Networking is the thing that will get you a good job. Use yours.

Succeed According to Your Own Standards

How do you define success? Does it mean being rich or powerful? Does it mean not having to work at all? Does it mean working in a job that you find fulfilling? Everyone has his or her own answer to this question. Success is highly individualized. The only definition that should matter to you is your own. It's fine to look at others and see what they have accomplished. You might even set your sights on similar goals. Learn from these people, but do not compare yourself to them using a mental scorecard. You are a unique person with your own life, your own characteristics, and your own sense of what success means to you.

FOCUS is crucial to your job search!

Taking Control

You cannot always control where your next home will be or what the job market will be like in that community. You might very well hit pay dirt and have a ton of job opportunities from which to choose. On the other hand, you might end up living in the middle of the desert with your closest job opportunities being miles away. Accept what you cannot control. You can, however, control your own actions. You can learn and apply the basic job search skills necessary for survival in today's job market, wherever that market may be located. Regardless of what anyone else says, if you are motivated, you can have a career or a job and be married to the military at the same time.

After all is said and done, perhaps the commercial had it right after all. You can be an army of one in life if you are armed with the right tools in the first place.

2

Begin At the Beginning

"The beginning is the most important part of the work." – Plato

PLATO COULD HAVE BEEN a military spouse who understood the job search process! Your job search begins with you. Why do you want to get a job? Is it something that you want to do for yourself? Do you need a job in order to make ends meet for yourself and for your family? What skills do you have to offer an employer? What kind of job would you like to have? Do you know what skills employers want or need? By taking the time to answer these questions, you will accomplish several important tasks. You will gain an increased awareness of what skills you actually have to offer an organization. This, in turn, will help you to better market yourself to employers. Your understanding of who you are and what you have to offer will be apparent in your resume, in your cover letters, and in your job applications. Let's face it. To be hired by employers, you have to first convince them that you are what they want. You have to sell your skills. To effectively sell your skills, you have to know who you really are and what you have to offer. There is an old saying that you will never get to where you want to go, unless you know where that is in the first place. In the end, it seems as though Plato was right.

What Do You Have to Offer?

Imagine that you are a salesperson who wants desperately to sell a product. How would you market that product? Would you plan a massive advertising campaign or a targeted one? What kind of information would you include in that advertising campaign? Of course, you would want to let people know about the features and capabilities of your product. Perhaps you want them to know about the product's history and versatility. Now, imagine that *you* are the actual product that you are trying to sell and the potential buyers are employers having positions they need to fill. What features and capabilities, or skills and abilities, do you have to offer? A good way to gather this information is to compile your career history on paper.

Compile Your Career History

If you've ever tried to piece together a puzzle without all the pieces, you'll understand the importance of compiling your career history. It is important to identify all of your skills – even the ones you may not want to use. Think of your career history as that puzzle. If you identify, organize, and add up the number of pieces you have, you'll be more likely to know where and when you can use them. For example, you will want to identify the jobs that you have held in the past. Be sure to include volunteer experiences as well as paid employment. Volunteer work is work experience regardless of whether you received a paycheck for it or not. What did you do in those positions? How long did you work there? Who was your supervisor? What was the address and telephone number of the company? Why did you stop working there? What about your education and training experiences? Do you have written documentation supporting your accomplishments? Did you ever receive any type of awards or certificates?

Put the hard-core facts of your work history under a magnifying glass and really examine what you've done. Admittedly, this is a time-consuming task. Do it anyway. Later, you will be glad that you did it. Use the worksheets on pages 9-12 to assist you in putting the pieces of your career puzzle together.

Work History

Complete the following information as much as possible. Try to go back at least ten years, if applicable, in your work history.

Job Title: _____ From _____ To _____

Company: _____

Address: _____

Telephone Number: _____

Supervisor: _____ Salary: _____

Responsibilities and Achievements: _____

_____

_____

_____

_____

_____

_____

_____

_____

_____

What I liked most about this job: _____

_____

_____

_____

_____

What I liked least about this job: _____

_____

_____

_____

_____

_____

Work History

Complete the following information as much as possible. Try to go back at least ten years, if applicable, in your work history.

Job Title: _____ From _____ To _____

Company: _____

Address: _____

Telephone Number: _____

Supervisor: _____ Salary: _____

Responsibilities and Achievements: _____

_____

_____

_____

_____

_____

_____

_____

_____

_____

What I liked most about this job: _____

_____

_____

_____

_____

What I liked least about this job: _____

_____

_____

_____

_____

_____

Work History

Complete the following information as much as possible. Try to go back at least ten years, if applicable, in your work history.

Job Title: _____ From _____ To _____
Company: _____
Address: _____
Telephone Number: _____
Supervisor: _____ Salary: _____

Responsibilities and Achievements: _____
_____
_____
_____
_____
_____
_____
_____
_____
_____

What I liked most about this job: _____
_____
_____
_____
_____

What I liked least about this job: _____
_____
_____
_____
_____
_____

Education and Training

Academic Education

☐ High School _____
           Name of School   Years Attended

☐ College _____
           Name of School   Years Attended

_____
           Name of School   Years Attended

_____
           Name of School   Years Attended

Significant Coursework: _____

☐ College (Graduate and Post-Graduate

_____
           Name of School   Years Attended

_____
           Name of School   Years Attended

Significant Coursework: _____

Training

_____
Course Title   Sponsor   Date Completed

_____
Course Title   Sponsor   Date Completed

_____
Course Title   Sponsor   Date Completed

_____
Course Title   Sponsor   Date Completed

_____
Course Title   Sponsor   Date Completed

Identify Your Skills

Your skills represent your unique abilities to accomplish tasks. You have developed them through a variety of experiences. There are three basic types of skills:

- self-management skills
- transferable or functional skills
- work content skills

1. Self-Management Skills

Self-management skills represent your personal traits. Some military spouses think that their personal traits do not affect their job search at all. That assumption, however, is a big mistake. Employers want to hire people who will fit into their organizations. "Fitting in" is personal in nature. Your self-management skills come heavily into play at this point. For example, are you an organized individual? Or are you more comfortable working in a state of disorganized chaos? Are you the type of person who would be willing to take a risk on the job, or would you rather play it safe? More than any other type of skill, self-management skills shed light on who you are as an individual.

Self-Management Skills Inventory

Read over the Self-Management Skills Inventory list on page 14 and circle the 10 skills that best describe you.

Self-Management Skills Inventory

accurate	consistent	imaginative
active	cooperative	independent
adaptable	courageous	industrious
adventurous	creative	innovative
aggressive	decisive	intelligent
alert	dedicated	intuitive
ambitious	dependable	inventive
analytical	detail-oriented	logical
artistic	determined	loyal
assertive	diligent	methodical
calm	direct	non-judgmental
candid	disciplined	open-minded
capable	eager	opportunistic
careful	efficient	organized
caring	energetic	perfectionist
cautious	enthusiastic	precise
charismatic	factual	reliable
clear-headed	fair-minded	responsible
clever	flexible	risk-taker
competitive	forceful	secure
concerned	friendly	self-motivated
concise	frugal	sensitive
confident	genuine	stable
conscientious	goal-oriented	talented
conservative	hardworking	trustworthy
considerate	honest	wise

Now let's make it even tougher. Look over the list again. Select the top five self-management skills that best describe you.

1. _____
2. _____
3. _____
4. _____
5. _____

2. Transferable or Functional Skills

Transferable skills, also known as functional, are mobile skills. They can easily travel between different types of jobs. For example, let's assume you work as a customer service representative in a bank.

- You interact daily with people.
- You explain the bank's services to potential customers.
- You set up accounts for customers.
- You resolve any problems that may arise with the accounts.

Now, suppose you want to open your own resume writing business. You will become a customer service representative of your own company.

- You may have to interact daily with people.
- You will explain your services to potential customers.
- You will set up customer accounts.
- You will resolve any problems that may arise with those accounts.

The jobs are different but the processes are the same. Functional skills, then, highlight processes that can be applied in different situations.

Army spouse, Chris Babich, a teacher, offers yet another example. Faced with zero luck in finding a teaching job in the competitive Northern Virginia job market, she decided to re-identify her skills. She knew that she could teach, and it was what she most enjoyed doing. She also loved taking aerobics classes. A light bulb went off in her head, and she decided to combine her two loves. She became a certified aerobics instructor. Her teaching skills *transferred* with her into a classroom of a different kind. Think about the things you most enjoy doing. Any light bulbs coming on in your mind yet?

The following list of transferable skills may help you.

Transferable Skills Inventory

Read over the following Transferable Skills Inventory list and circle 15 of the skills that you have used in the past.

adjust	drive	network
advise	edit	operate
alter	entertain	paint
analyze	evaluate	persuade
arrange	examine	plan
assess	follow up	post data
assist	formulate	problem solve
blend	guide	publicize
budget	handle	read
calculate	improvise	record
care for	include	refill
classify	influence	regulate
compare	inform	repair
compile	insert	report
compose	install	sell
compute	instruct	serve
conceptualize	interview	service
construct	invent	sew
consult	investigate	sort
cook	learn	supervise
coordinate	listen	synthesize
copy	manage	teach
create	manipulate	test
decorate	measure	type
demonstrate	mix	theorize
diagnose	motivate	transcribe
direct	negotiate	write

Take a closer look at those you've circled. Which ten of those do you most prefer to use?

Ten Transferable Skills I Most Prefer to Use

(List your favorites first)

1. _____
2. _____
3. _____
4. _____
5. _____
6. _____
7. _____
8. _____
9. _____
10. _____

3. Work Content Skills

Work content skills, also known as technical skills, are task-specific. They are the skills you must have in order to accomplish a given task. For example, if you are a computer programmer, you must know how to program computers. If you are a counselor, you must have counseling skills. If you are a cashier, you must know how to operate a cash register. Take a moment to think of all the jobs or assignments you have ever had. What specific technical skills do you have? Try to think of at least ten skills. If you can think of more than 10, write them in as well.

My Work Content Skills

1. _____
2. _____
3. _____
4. _____
5. _____
6. _____
7. _____
8. _____

9. _____

10. _____

Updating Your Skills

After taking a good, hard look at your work history, and your education and training experience, ask yourself if you need to update your skills or learn new ones. Even if you feel you have current marketable skills and abilities, realize that education is a lifelong process. It's something you should strive to incorporate into your life whether it involves formal classroom training or not.

There are several ways that you can gain new skills or update old ones:

- Enroll in a class at a local university or on-line.
- Contact the family services support or community service center on the military installation where you are stationed. Many centers offer free skills-based training.
- Volunteer your time to an organization in order to learn those skills.
- Teach yourself new skills.
- If you are employed, find out if your company will sponsor the training you want.

If you want to go back to school for a certificate or a degree, your first stop should be the education center located on the installation where you are stationed. Whether you are interested in finishing high school or beginning a doctorate degree, they can provide you with valuable information about educational opportunities located in your community.

The Money Issue

There's no denying that higher education and training cost money. That's an unfortunate fact of life. Don't let that stop you from advancing your career, however. If you want something badly enough, you can find a way to get it. If money is the only barrier between you and the education and training that you want, then get around it. How?

Depending upon your circumstances, you may be eligible for scholarship funding from a number of sources, including:

- Navy-Marine Corps Relief Society
- Non-Commissioned Officer's Association
- Air Force Aid Sergeants Association
- Fleet Reserve Association
- Officers and Non-Commissioned Officers Wives or Spouses Clubs
- Federal Government

In addition to military-related organizations, private corporations may even be able to help you with various scholarships.

Another answer to the "How do I find the money to go to college?" question is to target your job search toward companies that have tuition assistance benefits.

Two other places able to help you are the financial aid office at the school you are interested in attending and the education center on the military installation nearest you. Both organizations are well versed in identifying financial aid sources.

You also should check out various employment and training services available through hundreds of state One-Stop Career Centers. To locate the center nearest you, access the U.S. Department of Labor website:

www.doleta.gov/usworkforce/onestop/onestopmap.asp

Also, visit the U.S. Department of Labor's Service Locator:

www.servicelocator.org

The bottom line here? Learning is important. If you need or want certain skills to make yourself more marketable to employers, plan to get them one way or another.

Identifying Your Job Objective

Imagine your closet without any clothes hangers in it. The clothes lie on the floor in a pile. You have to practically sort through everything to find the one outfit you want to wear. By the time you find that outfit, you discover that it needs ironing from being crumpled on the floor. You waste precious time getting dressed because you didn't have your clothes hanging up properly. That is exactly how your job search looks without an objective statement. You fritter away time when you don't have a general direction in mind. You have a difficult time accessorizing your job search, because you don't have a basic theme going in the first place.

An *objective statement* is simply a single sentence that summarizes what it is that you want to do. You can have one objective statement or one hundred. It doesn't matter. Each objective, however, should be fully supported by actions that will help to make it become a reality.

Thinking of your ideal job may help you to formulate your objective statement. What are you doing? Where are you working? Are you interacting with other people, or do you see yourself sitting in front of a computer screen all day? Are you indoors or outside? Are you working independently or as a member of a close-knit team? What are the hours that you work? What do you like best about this perfect job? Now, write down your vision of your dream job in the space below.

Dream Job Sheet

Job Title:_____

Location:_____

Salary: _____

A typical day at work:_____

_____

_____

_____

_____

What I like best about this job:_____

_____

_____

_____

_____

Now, flip back to the worksheets you completed at the beginning of this chapter and compare them to your dream job sheet. Do you see any similarities? For example, did you list any skills on the dream job sheet that you have used in your real-life jobs? Which ones? Did you find any striking differences?

The following "I Want a Job..." list can help you further clarify your objective statement.

I Want a Job . . .

- ❑ that pays well and has excellent benefits.
- ❑ that is challenging and will allow me to advance.
- ❑ that encourages my creativity.
- ❑ that will reward me for a job well done.
- ❑ where I don't dread going to work every day.
- ❑ that is exciting and unpredictable.
- ❑ where my responsibilities are clearly defined.
- ❑ that will allow me to make decisions or have influence in the process.
- ❑ where I can be in charge of things.
- ❑ that involves taking calculated risks.
- ❑ that utilizes my skills and abilities to their fullest potential.
- ❑ where I don't have to be in charge of things.
- ❑ where I can be friends with my co-workers.
- ❑ that gives me the chance to travel occasionally.
- ❑ where I can work with different people all the time.
- ❑ where I don't have to work with different people all the time.
- ❑ that allows me flexibility in my work schedule.
- ❑ that doesn't interfere with my personal life.
- ❑ that is close to my home.
- ❑ that offers as much security as possible.
- ❑ where I might be able to transfer to different company locations.
- ❑ with a small business where I might be able to advance rapidly.
- ❑ where I can dress casually.
- ❑ where I must dress professionally at all times.
- ❑ that allows me to work independently of others.

Now it's time to develop your job objective, keeping in mind the factors that are important to you. Here are several examples:

- I want a position in the **retail industry** field as a **sales associate**.
- I want a position in the **administrative field** as an **office manager**.
- I want a position in the **education field** as an **undergraduate instructor**.
- I want a position in the **communications field** as a **technician**.
- I want a position in the **medical field** as a **physical therapist**.

Now you try it. Simply complete the following sentence:

I want a position in the _____ **field as a(n)** _____ **.**

Your objective statement is important. Use it as your mission statement. It is the goal of your immediate job search. In the next chapter, you will see that every job search action should fully support this statement.

Keep in mind that you may have to revise your objective depending upon your immediate needs and those of the job market.

Knowing What Employers Want

It's not enough to identify your priorities and skills. These items represent only a part of the job search equation. You also have to know what organizations want in their employees. One way to visualize what an employer may want is to put yourself in their place. If *you* were the employer looking to hire someone for a specific job, what skills and characteristics would you be looking for?

For example, if you wanted to hire an office manager, you might want these types of skills and characteristics a candidate:

- ❑ at least two years experience working as an office supervisor
- ❑ a high school degree or a GED
- ❑ computer literacy
- ❑ problem-solving skills
- ❑ good people management and communication skills

If you aren't sure what a specific job entails or what qualifications might be necessary, consult these Department of Labor resources:

- *Occupational Information Network (O*NET):* http://online.one tcenter.org. Here you will find brief job descriptions of over 1000 occupations that cover nearly 100% of the US workforce. Descriptions include personality type, work values, skills, abilities, general work activities, physical work conditions, experience, job preparation, and knowledge.

- *The Occupational Outlook Handbook (OOH):* www.bls.gov/oco/ home.htm. This resource provides you with information on roughly 250 occupations. It covers such areas as job duties, working conditions, training requirements, earnings potential, advancement possibilities, and sources of additional information.

- *The Career Guide to Industries (CG):* www.bls.gov/oco/cg Enables you to access career information by industry. There are over 42 industries covered. This guide serves as a companion to the *Occupational Outlook Handbook.*

- *The Occupational Outlook Quarterly (OOQ):* www.bls.gov/ opub/ooq.ooqhome.htm. Provides practical information on jobs and careers. Articles cover a wide variety of career and work-related topics such as new and emerging occupations, training opportunties, salary trends, and results of new studies from the Bureau of Labor Statistics.

Through information interviewing, you can talk to people working in the career fields that interest you. (See Chapter 8, "Interviewing With Ease," for more information.)

The three characteristics that employers most often seek in employees are:

1. **Ability** to do the job that has to be done.
2. **Willingness** to do the job that has to be done.
3. Ability to **fit** in their company.

Specifically, they want employees who:

- **have knowledge and the ability to learn.** Employers not only want their employees to have the old-fashioned skills of reading, writing, and arithmetic, but they also want employees who can conceptualize, plan, comprehend, and interpret data. Not surprisingly, employers also want people with computer skills. Computer literacy is a basic skill that you cannot fail to have. Familiarity with word processing, spreadsheet, database, and desktop publishing programs will increase your market value to a potential employer in need of those skills. Those who lack at least a basic understanding of computers are at a significant disadvantage in the job market.

- **possess solid decision-making skills.** Employers want people who are committed to their organization and who are not afraid to make decisions on their behalf. They want employees who can see what the existing and potential problems are and who can figure how ways to solve or prevent those problems.

- **can be flexible, adaptable, persistent, and can take the initiative necessary to see a task through to completion.** These are already characteristics of many military spouses. They represent "functional" skills that can easily be applied to the work environment.

- **can effectively communicate and work in teams.** The ability to communicate well is one of the most important skills that employers look for in job candidates. As an employee, you have to be able to work for and with others on many different professional levels.

- **can be assertive when necessary.** There is a fine line between being assertive and pushy. It's a fact that to get the job done, sometimes you have to be a little of both.

- **have professional networking skills and a familiarity with the company's history and goals.** As an employee of a particular company, you represent that company to the outside world. The more knowledge you have about it, its history, and its future goals, the more realistic your contribution can be to that organization.

Finding a Fit That Works for You

If you won't be satisfied until you find the perfect job, then there is a strong chance that you will never be satisfied. The perfect job doesn't exist. The key is to find a job that best meets your immediate needs and best supports your career objective. Depending upon your location and your unique situation, you may have to compromise along the way. For example, do you need a job in order to help meet basic living expenses? Then get that job. It may not even be close to your concept of the ideal job, but it will meet your needs for the moment. You can always discreetly continue your search for a better position.

You can always learn something from an experience even if that something means you do not ever want to do it again. Look for the value in everything you do and learn from it.

Don't be discouraged if you're not sure what it is that you want to do even after compiling your career history and identifying your skills. That's not unusual. All that means is that you might want to consider researching this particular area more. Your education center may be able to help you discover what it is that you want to do through the use of various assessment tools such as:

- Career Assessment Inventory
- Edwards Personal Preference Schedule
- Jackson Vocational Interest Survey
- Kuder Occupational Interest Survey
- Myers-Briggs Type Indicator
- Ramak Inventory
- Strong Interest Inventory
- Temperament and Values Inventory

These instruments are not designed to tell you what you should do. Only you can decide that. What they can do for you, however, is give you ideas that you may not have previously considered.

3

Planning for Success

"Success is more attitude than aptitude." – Unknown

ONTRARY TO WHAT WE MIGHT HOPE, a successful job search doesn't just happen; it's something that you have to work hard to achieve. It involves detailed planning, implementation, evaluation, and revision of your efforts. It's not always a fun thing, but it certainly is necessary.

The first step in your planning phase should involve looking to the end. What is it that you hope to achieve? A job? A career? An extra paycheck? Satisfaction? Knowing what you want in the end will make it much easier to ultimately obtain. The exercises in Chapter 2, "Begin at the Beginning," should have helped you analyze this part of the process.

Now on to the next stage...planning your success. It's common knowledge that the best qualified applicants don't always get hired. Often, the people who are hired are the ones who know the most about job hunting. These are the people who have taken the time to establish a plan. These are the people who actually implement, evaluate, and revise their plans as needed.

A number of activities are involved in this process and this chapter will seek to address them for you. Let's start with a story....

A Tale of Two Spouses

Once upon a time there were two military spouses who wanted to go to work. Each one took a very different approach to finding her respective job. The first spouse spent several weeks drafting and revising her resume, tweaking it to perfection. Finally, she laser printed out numerous copies of it and mailed them, along with a standard cover letter, to as many companies as she could locate. She and her husband were stationed near a large metropolitan area, so she felt quite confident that this approach would work just fine. After all, she was educated, experienced, and available. All she had to do now was wait and watch Oprah.

The second spouse did things differently. First of all, she and her husband were stationed at Fort NoWhere. Clearly, there were not many of opportunities available in this location. She knew this would demand more creativity and patience on her part. Adding to her situation was the fact that she did not have a college degree or much experience. She did, however, have determination, a great attitude, and this book to help her out. She committed herself to finding gainful employment by dedicating a consistent amount of time each day to achieving that goal. She drafted, revised, and finalized her resume within a few days. She contacted the family services center on post and the Department of Labor off post to learn about the local employers. Armed with that information, she snail-mailed and, in some cases, emailed her resume and individualized cover letters to potential employers. She also actively applied for specific openings which she learned about through her aggressive networking activities. While waiting for the interviews to be offered, she volunteered on post doing a job similar to the one she was trying to get on a salaried basis. While waiting, she kept her job search skills current and met new people who turned out to be instrumental in helping her finally become employed. Throughout the entire process, she kept her spirits up.

Which spouse, do you think, got it right?

Why You Need a Plan

The best laid plans often fail because people fail to plan properly. In other words, you need a plan if you want to find a decent job in a reasonable amount of time. Your plan doesn't have to be a complicated undertaking. It just has to have some type of focus to it. You can write it down on paper or keep it in your mind. Use whichever approach works better for you, but do it.

The Full Circle Job Search Plan

A full circle job search plan is a genuine strategy for success. It doesn't end when you get hired. It is a career management process that continues indefinitely. The basic components of a full circle job search plan include the following:

- Your Objective (what do you want to do?)
- Your Plan for Success (how are you going to do it?)
- Your Efforts: Identifying and Using Your Available Resources (do it)
- Your Evaluation and Revision of Those Efforts (if it doesn't work, fix it)

Having a plan is like having a camera with interchangeable lenses. With your wide angle lens you can get a good view of the big picture. By keeping track of what you do and revising your plan as necessary, or changing your lenses to a smaller size, you can see the finer details that go into the big picture.

A good plan details where you are now, where you want to be, and how you're going to get there. It doesn't have to written in stone, nor should it be. It should be a flexible plan which:

- establishes realistic goals
- tracks your actions and progress with an effective record-keeping system
- identifies your available resources
- contains built-in measures to beat the job search blues if and when they strike

Your Objective

In Chapter 2, "Begin at the Beginning," you drafted an objective statement. In its simplest form, that is what you are striving to do, and it becomes the basis for your plan as well.

Writing Your Objective Statement

Example:
My objective is to work as a management analyst in the quality assurance field.

Your turn:
My objective is to work as a/an _____
in the _____ field.

Your Plan for Success

Congratulations, you have your objective in place. Now it's time to figure out what actions you need to take in order to make that objective a reality. Specifically, it's time to get down to business and do the following:

- Identify and research potential employers and available resources
- Find out about real and projected job openings
- Apply for those positions
- Interview for positions
- Follow up your actions throughout the whole process.
- Accept and negotiate a job offer or continue your search (or both)

Your Efforts: Identifying and Using Your Available Resources

Your available resources are varied and forever changing. You should know what is available in your local and global community in order to take full advantage of their offerings. Let's take a brief look at some of the services available for your use within the military and civilian communities.

Department of Defense

The Department of Defense (DoD) is more than aware that spousal employment is a critical issue having a great impact on the quality of life experienced by service members and their families. That makes it an important issue to the DoD because satisfied service members usually stay in the military. Those who are dissatisfied, leave when their time is up, creating a loss of qualified employees who were not cheap to train in the first place. A 1999 Active Duty Member Survey of the Defense Manpower Data Center revealed, not surprisingly, that members with spouses who were employed in civilian jobs (54.5%) or voluntarily out of the workforce (55%) indicated greater satisfaction with the military way of life than did other married personnel. Other surveys found that when spouses were employed and earning more, then they were more likely to be satisfied with the military lifestyle and this in turn increased the chances that their active duty spouses would remain in the service.

As a result of such findings, each of the military departments has numerous initiatives relating to spouse employment. One such DoD-wide initiative is PL 107-107, Section 571, which is the final version of House Resolution (HR) 2413, The Military Spouse Employment Assistance Act of 2001. Introduced in June 2001, it includes such elements as the following:

- A three-year DoD pilot program to provide financial assistance to military spouses for job-related costs such as education, skill certification, teacher's license fees, job-hunting trips, and counseling.
- A requirement for DoD contractors to give priority to military spouses in the employment selection process.
- A close working relationship between DoD and other federal agencies, chambers of commerce, and industry, to help provide jobs and job search assistance.

Military Family Service and Support Centers

As a military spouse, you have access to organizations that exist to help you find employment. They are as close to you as your nearest military installation:

- Navy Family Services Centers
- Marine Corps Family Services Centers
- Air Force Family Support Centers
- Coast Guard Work Life Programs
- Army Community Service Centers
- Transition Assistance Centers in all the services

Their programs and services are invaluable and diverse. They are your instant network, regardless of where you happen to be stationed. Call them for assistance at your new station before you even arrive there. For information on these centers, see "the Red, White and Blue Pages" at the end of this book.

Employment Readiness Programs

Family support and service centers throughout all branches of the military sponsor employment readiness programs (previously called family member employment assistance programs) for military spouses. Specifically, these programs may be able to offer you:

- Individualized job search assistance
- Resume, job application, and cover letter critiques
- Access to local and federal job listings
- Job referrals to employers
- Access to computers for word processing and online activities as well as access to the archaic typewriter which still comes in handy every now and then
- Opportunities to keep your skills current via volunteering assignments
- Free job skills training
- Access to locally organized job clubs

Transition Assistance Programs (TAP)

Transition assistance programs are an excellent resource for the job seeker. Unfortunately, the programs may be limited to servicing only military personnel and their families who are transitioning out of the military, or to civilian employees who are subjected to a reduction in force. Even those individuals are only eligible to use the programs for a limited time period. This does periodically change and can differ from installation to installation. It is definitely worth a phone call to them to see if you are eligible to use their services. Perhaps you and your spouse are in the process of transitioning out of the military. Take advantage of the services offered by the TAP, including:

- Individual transition counseling
- Job search strategy seminars and workshops
- Access to computer and dedicated career software
- Access to photocopy machines, faxes and telephones for local calls.

The Army is unique in that their TAP includes the Army Career and Alumni Program (ACAP), which provides job search assistance and facilitates the completion of the DD 2648, Individual Transition Checklist (a form required of service members prior to separating from the military). The ACAP website (www.acap.army.mil), however, can be accessed by anyone and has tons of good information and helpful job search links. For contact information regarding transition assistance centers and ACAPs worldwide, visit this website: dod.transportal.org.

Family Support Groups (FSGs)

Family support groups were designed to assist family members in dealing with issues that often arise when the service member is deployed to places afar. Many units throughout the services have organized groups in place. Some groups are more active than others, but they represent an excellent opportunity to establish invaluable networking contacts.

Professional Associations and Clubs

The hidden job market is alive and well within professional associations or clubs. Many job vacancies go unannounced because they are filled through these avenues. Here is a short list of military-related groups:

- Non-Commissioned Officer's Wives Club
- Officers' Wives and Civilian Clubs
- Non-Commissioned Officers' Association
- Military Officers' Association of American (MOAA)
- Federal Women's Program
- American Legion
- Veterans of Foreign Wars

In addition to those mentioned above, consider joining a professional or trade association in your career field. For example, trainers would find membership in the American Society for Training and Development useful. Being a member of professional organizations generally gives you access to the membership directories – in other words, an instant network of people with similar interests who are usually willing and able to assist fellow members in finding employment.

College Career Services Office

If you are enrolled in undergraduate or graduate level coursework, you might have a career services office available to you, depending upon the location of your school. Use it. It can provide you with a great service, free of charge. If you're not sure what you want to be when you grow up, they can help. If you need help creating a resume and want to know how to interview successfully for a job, they can help you with that, too. Even if you don't attend the school, their services might still be available to you for a small fee.

Department of Labor (DoL)

Often known as the unemployment office, the Department of Labor can be a great resource for you. Apply for jobs through this office at no charge to you. Many companies will only list their vacancies through the DoL to save themselves from the screening process. Look into potential unemployment benefits while you are here.

Chamber of Commerce

The mission of a chamber of commerce is to bring business to the community. This is an excellent place to learn about your new area and potential employers. Check out these websites:

- U.S. National Chamber of Commerce: www.2chambers.com
- National Black Chamber of Commerce: www.nationalbcc.org
- International Chamber of Commerce: www.iccwbo.org

Employment Agencies Found in the Yellow Pages

Apply for temporary and permanent positions through area no-fee employment agencies. Many employers have exclusive contracts with these agencies to do their hiring. There are also agencies which charge you for their services. Word of advice....stick with the no-fee agencies.

Newspapers

Read the business section to get the low-down on local happenings. Read the want ads, of course. Don't, however, focus your whole search on them. For online access to thousands of newspapers, visit these websites:

www.newspaperlinks.com
www.newspapers.com

Your Evaluation and Revision of These Efforts

It is critical that you continuously re-evaluate and revise your plan as you go along. Circumstances change. Job opportunities aren't always there waiting for you. Sometimes you end up taking a less than perfect job because it may be all that is available at the time and you choose not to remain unemployed. Objectives change. Maybe you've decided that you want to do something totally different. It's quite all right to change career paths. Your plan should change to keep up with the reality of these factors.

Establishing Realistic Goals

Which goal is more realistic?

    A. I will get a job.
    B. I will apply for three jobs today.

Obviously, "B" is the right answer. "A" is a goal; however, it is too vague. It doesn't give details. Details are the stuff that makes things happen and your goals should explicitly include them. Specific details, or baby steps, are critical to the achievement of your goals. It is best to state them clearly and concisely.

Keeping Track of What You Do

Imagine for a moment that you have been tirelessly job hunting for a month. You have completed countless application forms, emailed and mailed dozens of resumes to prospective employers, and smiled until your cheekbones felt like they were going to fall off. You drag yourself home one night and turn on your voice mail. There is a promising message regarding an interview from someone named

Cindy. She wants you to call her as soon as possible. In her excitement, she did not leave a phone number or the name of her company (assuming she is actually calling from one). It can happen. How are you going to call her back? You have talked to so many people in the last month that you may or may not remember her.

This type of situation isn't a problem for someone who keeps track of his or her job search activity. Details, once again, matter and it's crucial that you record them for three good reasons:

1. It will help you remember which companies and people you have already contacted, to avoid being a nuisance to potential employers and to avoid making yourself look incompetent.

2. It will allow you effectively monitor your progress.

3. It will help you keep track of names and numbers so you don't have to store everything in your short-term memory.

What is the best way to organize and track your progress? This will largely depend on you and your style of managing information. If you are a natural born organizer, this will be easy for you. If, however, organization isn't your strongest suit, you will need to make the extra effort in this department.

Electronic Organizers

Electronic handheld organizers, also known as PDAs (Personal Digital Assistants), are marvelously convenient. They can be tucked into your coat pocket or purse, and you can update actions as they occur, keeping details fresh in your mind.

Paper Organizers

If you are more a see-it-on-paper type of person, the following blank form may be helpful to you:

The Activity Tracker

Target Company: _____

Address: _____

Telephone: _____

Fax: _____

Email: _____

Main Contacts: _____

_____

_____

Remarks: _____

_____

_____

_____

_____

Date   Activity

_____

_____

_____

_____

_____

_____

_____

Index Cards

In lieu of an electronic organizer or a blank form, simple index cards are an excellent way to keep track of your contacts. Use one card per company and keep it updated with your efforts.

ABC Company, 1515 First Avenue (555) 555-5555
Dave James, Personnel Manager
Cindy Jones, Graphic Arts Department Manager

3/2/03 — Workout with Cindy at gym and she suggested I send in resume. There may be an opening in the personnel dept soon.

3/3/03 — Rec'd call from Mr. James today and an interview has been set up for this Friday at 9am.

Old Fashioned Spiral Notebooks or Folders

Keep track of all those extra sheets of paper that seem to turn up in a job search. Invest in a spiral notebook or folder and file your documentation there. For example, you might keep in this notebook a disk containing your job search files. You might also keep a hard copy of your resume and any company literature (i.e., business cards, leaflets, material downloaded from the Internet) you've accumulated in your search.

Managing Your Time

It would be quite easy to spend the majority of your time organizing your job search. You don't have to take any risks when you are organizing. There is no rejection associated with surfing the Internet job boards or revising your resume. There is, however, a real danger involved in spending too much time planning your job search and not enough time actually searching. Even a perfect job search plan will fail if you neglect to implement it. You must go out into the cruel, cruel world and find out about openings. You must actually apply for them and try to convince total strangers that you are perfect for their companies. Job hunting is not a task for the tenderhearted. It means you must always propel your efforts forward by spending a consistent amount of time on a daily basis toward achieving your goal.

In this whole process, it's easy to confuse your job search with your life search. Keep in mind that you already have a life; you are simply looking for a job (perhaps a meaningful job, but a job nonetheless). Don't make the mistake of neglecting the other, more important, parts of your life.

Avoiding the Job Search Blues

Just when you least expect it, they hit. The job search blues are a fact of life and it's critical that you know how to deal with them in advance. Here are some helpful suggestions for banishing the rejection blues:

- No matter how great you are, you will hear "no" at one point or another. Don't take it personally. "No" doesn't mean that you are a bad person. It doesn't mean that your skills are worthless. It just means no. It means that a particular opportunity isn't going to work out for you for whatever reason.

- Get plenty of rest each night. A good night's sleep can be motivating, refreshing, and downright healthy.
- Eat right. At the risk of sounding like your mother, eat healthy foods. Remember, garbage in, garbage out.
- Exercise. Walk the kids, the dog, or yourself. Jog. Hit the post or base gym. Do something constructive besides nothing to alleviate the inevitable job search stress.
- Do other things in your life besides look for work. Strive for some type of balance in your life. Remember, you are looking for a job, not a life. You already have a life!
- Do something nice for someone else. It sounds old-fashioned, but it really works. Try it.
- Develop your own encouraging mantra and repeat it to yourself throughout the day, particularly when you're feeling down.
- Read a good book for the fun of it. Whether you crave junk food for the mind or intellectual stimulation, a good read can provide a little harmless escapism.
- Introduce yourself to the new neighbor. If there is one thing a military spouse understands, it is how it feels to be the new person on the block. Perhaps you could make that person feel welcome and make a new friend or networking contact at the same time.
- Do something nice for yourself. Shop. Golf. Get a massage. Whatever. Treat yourself well. You deserve it.

Achieving Success

If searching for a job were easy, no one would write books to help millions of job seekers land that coveted job. And for those married to the military the process is even harder. But if you follow the suggestions in this chapter and those that follow, you will give yourself a leg up on attaining your goal of career management and satisfaction while moving from base to base.

4

Options
That Work

FINDING A JOB WILL BE a lot easier if you know where
to look for opportunities in the first place. You might think
that your options are limited because of your mobile
lifestyle, but that simply is not true. The military is not alone in
moving its employees all over the United States and abroad. Today,
more than ever, America's workforce is mobile. Your options for
employment are the same as anyone else's. In fact, your options might
even be greater because of your varied experiences. Consider the following options:

- Federal Employment – Appropriated Funds
- Federal Employment – Non-appropriated Funds
- Defense Contracting
- Military Exchange System
- Self-Employment
- Private Industry
- Opportunities Abroad
- Volunteering

Federal Employment -
Appropriated Funds

Your spouse works for Uncle Sam. Why shouldn't you? Fortunately, it is not as difficult as it used to be to apply for jobs. The Office of Personnel Management (OPM), the human resources agency of the federal government, now touts a simple "3-Step Process."

STEP 1: Explore federal job opportunities either by accessing OPM's website at www.usajobs.opm.gov or by telephone 24/7 at 1-478-757-3000.

STEP 2: Locate a job that interests you. The website mentioned in Step 1 posts agency vacancy announcements, including job locations, duties, salaries, necessary education and experience, and complete application instructions.

STEP 3: Apply for the job. Clear instructions regarding application procedures are outlined within each vacancy announcement. The OPM website also lets you:

- learn about job vacancies worldwide
- read employment fact sheets
- obtain job applications and forms online
- build your federal resume and transmit it online
- apply for some positions online as well

Once you find a position that you are interested in, read the vacancy announcement carefully. It is crucial that you read the entire announcement and understand it, as dry as it may seem to you. There are a number of areas that could make a difference in your chances for employment.

For example, you may be the perfect person for that job, but you may not be eligible to apply for it. Paying particular attention to the "Areas of Consideration" paragraph will tell you if you can apply or not. Also pay close attention to the "Closing Date," which can mean one of two things. Either you have to have your application emailed or postmarked by or on that date, or it must actually be received by the hiring agency by or on that date. Finally, the

"How to Apply" paragraph is significant, too. You may have to apply using one of the following:

- an OF 612, Optional Employment Application Form
- a federal resume (that you create by yourself or with the assistance of a resume builder)
- SF 171, Standard Employment Application Form

In addition to one of the above forms or resume, you may be required to submit additional supporting documentation such as:

- a set of self-described Knowledge, Skills and Abilities (KSAs) as requested by the specific announcement.
- proof of your preference claim (i.e., a copy of your spouse's military orders if you are claiming military spouse or family member preference, or a copy of your DD 214 if you are prior military and claiming veteran's preference).

Pros of Working for the Government

- Salary levels are fairly competitive with private industry.
- Civil servants having career status receive great excellent benefits, including a generous paid vacation program and a savings plan with matching contributions.
- Federal jobs generally exist where military members are stationed, making this an attractive option for spouses who choose to relocate with their active duty spouses.
- Spouses can use their "military spouse preference" to help them obtain employment.
- It's difficult to get fired from a federal position.

Cons of Working for the Government

- The federal government, believe it or not, is smaller; therefore, the opportunities for employment have decreased.
- Many employees will remain on the job, making it difficult for new hires to come on board.
- Military spouses often find themselves underemployed with the federal government (meaning they are qualified for technical or managerial positions, but are only able to get hired in the lower paying clerical field).
- Many times spouses can only get hired on a temporary, part-time or seasonal basis without any benefits.

- Fairly or not, managers will often select a spouse who appears to have a longer availability than one who appears near a permanent change of station (PCS) move. ("Appears" is used here, because we all know that you can move every two years or be stuck in the same place for ten).

Competitive and Excepted Services

There are two classes of jobs within the federal government: competitive civil service and excepted service. **Competitive civil service jobs** fall under the jurisdiction of OPM and are subject to civil service laws passed by Congress to ensure fair and equal treatment in the hiring process. Selecting officials are given broad authority to review and select the best-qualified candidates based on job-related criteria.

Excepted service jobs are associated with agencies, such as the Federal Bureau of Investigations (FBI), the Central Intelligence Agency (CIA) and certain organizations within other agencies, set their own qualification requirements and are not subject to the appointment, pay, and classification rules in title 5, United States Code. They are subject to veterans' preference, however.

Military Spouse Preference (MSP)

As a military spouse, you are entitled to claim "military spouse preference" (MSP) when applying for a federal position. This is a preference that provides priority in the employment selection process for spouses who are relocating as a result of their military spouses permanent change of station (PCS). It can be used for most vacant positions with the Department of Defense (DoD) and it applies only within the commuting area of the permanent duty station where the sponsor is stationed. It is only available with the DoD. It is a preference, not a guarantee, of employment. Nor is it a special type of employment appointment. If you are claiming military spouse preference, you must still be the best qualified applicant for the job in the first place and you must present proof of your eligibility to claim it.

Spouse preference begins 30 days prior to your sponsor's reporting date to the new duty station and continues until you accept a position or decline an interview for a position.

This program may be operated differently from installation to installation. How it is applied depends upon several factors to include how a vacancy is being filled, its location and whether or not you are immediately "appointable." Generally, you are only able to use it once per duty station. There may be exceptions to this in different regions, and it is vital that you clarify how the preference is used in your area. (For example, in Germany, within United States Army Europe or USAREUR, you may be able to use it again even after you've accepted a temporary position.) For regulatory guidance concerning this preference, consult DoD Instruction 1404.12, Employment of Spouses of Active Duty Military Stationed Worldwide. Check out this website for more information on the Spouse Preference Program: www.cpms.osd.mil/vip/per_data/6314.htm.

Family Member Preference (FMP)

Family member preference (FMP) is also a DoD employment preference for eligible family members residing with a member of the U.S. Armed Forces or a U.S. citizen civilian employee of a U.S. government agency, whose duty station is in a foreign area. Again, having this preference does not guarantee employment and it is not applicable for hiring authorities. FMP is only available within the DoD.

For more information regarding federal employment, visit the U.S. Office of Personnel Management website: www.opm.gov. You could also contact your local Civilian Personnel Advisory Center (CPAC). These centers usually exist on or near the installation where the jobs are physically located.

Non-Appropriated Fund Positions

Non-appropriated fund (NAF) positions are also government jobs. Unlike civil service jobs, however, the salaries for NAF positions are paid from locally generated Morale, Welfare and Recreation (MWR) activities. NAF jobs are typically customer service oriented positions ranging from entry to managerial levels. Many NAF work schedules demand part-time, intermittent, or shift work. To learn about NAF positions, contact your local NAF personnel office. Many NAF openings are also posted online with the installation's main web page.

You are also able to use your military spouse preference for consideration of NAF employment. If you accept a NAF job using your spouse preference, then that acceptance of employment satisfies your use of the preference program. In other words, you can't accept a NAF job using your military spouse preference and then turn around and use your military spouse preference to gain employment for a civil service job.

Defense Contracting

Defense contracting is a great option for military spouses. You might be surprised by how many contractors are on your base. Among them are:

- Bank and credit union employees
- Transition center employees
- Education center employees
- Computer technicians at the telecommunications center
- Network planners and their support staff
- Payroll specialists
- Aircraft and weapons technicians

More and more of the military is being contracted out, and those jobs have to be filled by people having the right qualifications.

The Top 10 Defense Contractors, 2001

Rank	Company
1	Lockheed Martin Corp.
2	The Boeing Co.
3	Northrop Grumman Corp.
4	Raytheon Co.
5	General Dynamics Corp.
6	United Technologies Corp.
7	Science Applications International Corp.
8	TRW Inc.
9	Health Net Inc.
10	L-3 Communications Holdings Inc.

Military Exchange System

The next time you find yourself shopping at the post exchange (PX) or base exchange (BX), take a good look around you. You will no doubt see cashiers, store managers, customer service representatives, office personnel, warehouse workers, stockers, and vendors. Not only is your exchange a great place to shop for things, it is a great place to shop for jobs, too. Employees of the military exchange systems also have military spouse hiring preference at other exchanges, which can be helpful when you move from place to place. Procedures for applying may vary from store to store, but count on having to complete an employment application form. Resumes are generally not required, but may be submitted in addition to the application form.

For job opportunities within the Army and Air Force
Exchange Service (AAFES):
http:www.aafes.com.

For job opportunities within the Navy Exchange Service:
http:www.navy-nex.com/exchange/index.html

Self-Employment

The thought of being your own boss almost sounds too good to be true. Set your own hours. Work in your bunny slippers. Take Fridays and Mondays off. The reality of self-employment, however, is often a different story. Generally speaking, people who are their own bosses usually work longer hours and harder than those who punch clocks or sign timecards. It is an endeavor for someone who is ambitious, self-confident, and willing to commit the long hours and hard work necessary to make things happen. Indeed, the 40-hour a week job may even begin to look glamorous to the poor soul working 80 hours to turn a profit. To be self-employed, you should:

- have excellent organizational skills
- have superior people skills
- thrive on responsibility and independence
- have a truly supportive spouse

If this is an option that you are seriously considering, you might want to select a business that can travel with you when you move, assuming that the military likes to send you and your spouse packing every few years. Ideas for such portable careers are limited only to your imagination, but here is a short list to get you thinking:

- accounting
- computer programming
- consulting
- decorating
- entertaining
- gardening
- instructing
- planning and organizing
- repairing
- sewing
- tutoring
- web page design
- word processing
- writing

Helpful Small Business Websites	
www.sba.gov	US Small Business Administration
www.sba.gov/sbdc	Small Business Development Centers
www.score.org	Service Corps of Retired Executives
www.irs.gov	Internal Revenue Service
www. Entrepreneur-america.com	Rob Ryan's Entrepreneur America
www.Entreworld.com	Kauffman Center for
	Entrepreneurial Leadership
www.Homeworkingmom.com	Mothers' Home Business Network
www.Womensbusinessresearch.org	Center for Women's Business Research

If you live in base or post housing and wish to start your own business, check with the local installation first. You may or may not be allowed to do so. If you are able to have your own business in your quarters, you will need to comply with installation regulations as well as city, state and federal laws. For example, you may not be allowed to sell products but you may be allowed to sell services.

You might also be prohibited from using your military post office box as a business mailing address.

If you are stationed overseas, living in military housing and wish to open your own business, it gets even more complicated (not impossible, however). In addition to having the permission of the installation commander, you will also need to comply with American and host nation regulatory agencies (i.e., federal, state, city taxing authorities, to name a just a few). In Germany, for example, you would also be subject to obeying North Atlantic Treaty Organization (NATO) Status of Forces Agreement (SOFA) laws as well as those of Germany. Because of customs regulations, you would not be permitted to sue your military privileges for your private business purposes (i.e., you couldn't use the post exchange to buy your office supplies or use your military registered vehicle in your business at all). Additionally, you would be responsible for paying German taxes such as the *einkommensteur* (income tax), the *umstzsteuer* (turnover tax), and the *gewerbesteuer* (state income tax equivalent). This is not an attempt to discourage you at all. This is just a heads up to you about the different types of details that you have to consider.

Regardless of where you are stationed and living, if you are contemplating starting your own business, pay a visit to the legal office. They can give you information, free of charge, that could end up saving you a lot of heartache down the road. The better you plan for your own business, just as you would your job search, the better chance you have for success.

Private Industry

Outside the main gate of the installation where you are stationed, there is a world. It is either a big one that would survive without a hiccup should your installation go away or one that revolves around the military. In either case, private industry is a common factor of each and it is a wonderful option for you, the job seeker. As discussed in Chapter 3, "Planning for Success," make it a point to visit your local Department of Labor, Chamber of Commerce, and the area no-fee employment agencies in the area to find out about local industry and opportunities. Couple this with your independent efforts to research and contact employers and you'll find yourself employed in no time!

For a list of the major Internet job boards advertising job opportunities within private industry, refer to the Red, White and Blue Pages at the end of this book.

Opportunities Abroad

What happens when you want or have to work and you get orders for Germany, England, Italy, Greece, Korea, or Turkey? Never fear. There is hope and employment overseas for military spouses. Granted, opportunities may be greater for you in Germany than they would be for you in Greece, but they do exist. Handle your job search for employment overseas just as you would for employment in the good old U.S. Plan for it. Research it. Do it. The Internet takes away any excuses for not knowing about your next duty station and the potential job opportunities that may exist there. Many of the major job boards also list international positions as well. A good online resource for mobile spouses living abroad is Going Global: www.goinglobal.com.

Volunteering

Another option that may work for you is volunteering. It has several advantages:

- It allows you to keep your skills current.
- It provides you an opportunity to network in your field.
- It gives you the opportunity to learn new skills and gain experience in a given area.
- It may open the door for future paid employment within the same organization.
- It can keep you from becoming complacent about your job search or career.

To reap the real benefits from volunteering, you must do it with some degree of regularity and with a definite degree of commitment. Contact your installation volunteer coordinator through the family services or support center to inquire about available positions within the military community. You can always contact the employer where you want to volunteer directly for further guidance.

Use Your Imagination

Your employment options are limited by one thing and one thing only – your own imagination. If you should happen to overhear other spouses complain about the lack of job opportunities within the community, realize that their imaginations may not be as adventuresome, flexible, or as motivated as yours, and they may not have read this book!

5

Job Search
Power Tools

FINDING A GOOD JOB in a reasonable amount of time is easy if you use a variety of job search power tools effectively. These tools do not have power cords or on and off switches. You don't have to be careful using them around water (unless the job you want happens to be in or around the water itself). You should, however, keep these tools fully charged and ready for action at all times...even after you're happily employed.

Your power tools will work more effectively for you on your job search project if you use them in concert with one another. For example, networking is, without any doubt, the best way to find a job. It is not the only way, though. Combine networking with an Internet job search and other more traditional techniques and you can't lose. What you will do is generate more choices for yourself and that's what it is really all about...having a choice in the matter. No one likes to feel like she has to settle for anything. You don't have to settle at all. Get what you want and make it happen by pulling out your power tools and getting down to business. Specifically, you'll want to make sure you have these tools primed and ready:

- Your network
- Your references

- Your communication skills
- Your internet job search skills
- Your traditional job search skills
- Your mindset
- Your follow-up

Networking: Is Your Net Working?

You have probably heard the old saying that it's not what you know, but whom you know that counts. Like it or not, that's the way it is in the real world. Fortunately, you can network with anyone. Anyone means just that...*anyone*. You can network with your spouse, your friends, or your babysitter. You can network with your neighbors or with the crowd at the gym. You can even network with total strangers whom you stand in line with at the commissary or at the bank. Anyone can help you. Anyone can have influence. That's the beauty of it.

The key to making your "net" work for you is to realize that you have one in the first place and to nurture it. With a little care and tenderness, it will grow and so will your opportunities for employment. Make a written list of everyone you know who might be able to help you. Don't limit the list to people who are stationed at the same installation as yourself. Some military spouses make this mistake and it is a big one. Think about all the places you have been stationed and all the people you have met along the way. How many people are on your Christmas card list? You might very well have an incredibly extensive network already in place. You just may not be using it to its fullest power.

Another effective technique is to tell everyone with whom you come into contact on a daily basis that you are in the market for a new job. Ask them to keep their ears and eyes open for you and ask them if they can refer you to someone else who could be helpful. If you feel funny doing this, try to get over it. Remember, a good network is not one that you only take away from. It is one that you give back to, as well. People can help you and you can help others.

Whom You Can Network With

- Spouse and his/her colleagues
- Other family members
- Current and former employers
- Current and former co-workers
- Friends
- Fellow associates through church and community activities
- Acquaintances
- Service people (anyone you pay monthly bills to)
- Current or former teachers (your own or your kids)
- Fellow professional organization members
- Former classmates and alumni associations

Networking Contacts

Name/Relationship	Telephone	Email

Your References:
How to Take Good Care of Them

In deciding whether to hire you, employers may base part of their decision on what your references say about you. What is the moral of this story? Choose your personal and professional references with extreme care.

You can have as many references as you like; however, three to five is generally adequate at a given time. Select three people who know you on a professional level, such as past employers, co-workers, or associates. Select two individuals who know you on a personal level. It is best to avoid asking family members to be your personal references unless the employer specifically asks for that information. Don't worry if your references are not located in the same place that you are stationed. Location is not the important issue. What is important is that your references know you well and can say positive things about you.

Draft your list of potential key references below. The list might have more than five or as many as 20. That's fine. Just don't use them all at the same time or over-use them. Draw from your pool of references to pick the best ones for a given situation.

My Potential References

Name/Relationship	Telephone	Email
Professional:		
Ray Smith — current supervisor ABC Co, Inc.	(555) 555-5555	rsmith@email.com
Joe Vick — past supervisor	(555) 555-5555	jvick@email.address
Bonnie Jaques — co-worker	(555) 555-5555	bjq@email.address
Personal:		
Sherry Clevenger — Former co-worker	(555)555-5555	sherry@email.address
Sharon Phillips — Professor	(555) 555-5555	sphillips@email.address

---

Once you've selected your references, you need to contact them personally. First, ask them for permission to use their names in vain. Will they agree to be your references? If they agree, ask them what they would actually say about you should a potential employer call and ask them. This is important. After you hear what they say, you may or may not want them on your reference list. Second, you want to give your resume to each person who agrees to be a reference. You need to keep them informed about what it is you are trying to accomplish and the type of job you are seeking. Network with them. Don't overuse any particular person's name. Treat your references with the same consideration you would a potential employer.

Finally, you should also have a written reference sheet, suitable to give to a potential employer should the occasion arise. "References Available Upon Request" means that you really do have them available upon request. Such a document should be printed on the same type of paper as your resume (assuming a hard copy) and in a similar format. It should include your heading and the contact information of your references: each person's name, job title, company, address, telephone, email, and relationship to you. It might be similar to the example on page 55.

Your Name

Address

City, State, Zip

(555) 555-5555

youremail.address

REFERENCES

Professional

Ray Smith, Manager
ABC Co., Inc.
555 West End Avenue
Clarksville, Tennessee 55555
(555) 555-5555
rsmith@email.address
Relationship: Current Supervisor

Bonnie Jaques, Payroll Specialist
Defense Finance & Accounting Center
Building 55555
Patrick's Air Force Base, Florida 55555
(555) 555-5555
bjq@email.address
Relationship: Former co-worker

Joe Vick, Personnel Supervisor
U.S. Air Force
Building 55555
Fort Carson, Colorado 55555
(555) 555-5555
jvick@email.address
Relationship: Former supervisor

Personal

Dr. Sharon Phillips
Community College of the Air Force
555 Academic Avenue
APO AE 55555
(555) 555-5555
sphillips@email.address
Relationship. Friend

Sherry Clevenger
55555 San Martin Avenue
Nashville, Tennessee 55555
(555) 555-5555
sherry@email.address
Relationship: Friend

Your Communication Skills: It's How You Say It, Too

It's a given that you must be able to represent yourself effectively and professionally in a resume or cover letter. Equally important is the fact that you must also be able to communicate clearly face-to-face, over the telephone, or via email.

Face-to-Face: Creating a Sales Sound Bite

There's no getting around it. You must be able to speak confidently and intelligently about your skills and abilities to a potential employer or to anyone in a position to help you find a job. This isn't easy for many people. Developing and practicing a sales sound bite will make this task less awkward.

A sound bite is a verbal resume or a sales pitch that can be used in a number of different circumstances.

To develop your own sound bite, be familiar with who you are as a person and what you have to offer an employer. Your sound bite should contain relevant information such as:

- Your experience as it relates to that company or that person's interest
- Two or three highlights of skills or strengths that you could bring to the company or organization.
- Any significant accomplishments that you've achieved.
- Any applicable training or education you've completed.
- A high-impact closing that shows you know something about the company besides its name.

Your sound bite should not be a one-hour dissertation about wonderful you. It should be a relatively short blurb that you can use in a variety of situations. You can use it in a job interview when you're asked to tell the employer about yourself. You can use it during a fact-finding telephone call to a potential employer. You can use it on the person sitting next to you at your daughter's soccer game.

Here is a sample sound bite:

> Hello, my name is Rhonda Wells. For the past seven years, I have worked in the human resources field as a job assistance specialist. It is more than just a job to me; it is something I love to do. I understand, through mutual acquaintances, that you may want to hire a personnel supervisor in the near future. I would be interested in applying for the position. As an experienced supervisor, trainer, and counselor, I feel that I could bring many good qualities to your organization. I have a bachelor's degree in Business and Management. I find the personnel field fascinating because it involves people and their lives. I like making a positive difference in the lives of others. I know that your company has an excellent reputation locally as well as on a nationwide level. May I send my resume over to you today?

Over the Telephone

The telephone can be a terrific job search tool to use, if you follow some basic guidelines:

- Know what you want to get out of the phone call before you even pick up the receiver. Is your goal to obtain information about a particular job or a company? Do you want to find out who the decision-maker is within an organization? Do you want to find out what jobs are currently available?

- Prepare a written telephone script that includes all the questions on it that you want to ask. This way you won't forget anything while you're busy chatting away.

- Be considerate of the person on the other end of the telephone. Ask if he has the time to speak with you before you launch into your script. If you call at an inconvenient time, ask when you could call back.

- Do not leave messages for others to call you back. Simply find out when you should call back yourself.

- If you are having bad luck reaching a specific person because of overprotective support staff, then try calling back at odd hours. For example, try phoning before eight in the morning or after five in the evening.

telephone. You don't have the advantage of watching body language, so you need to get a feel for the mood of the person somehow.

- Don't call someone when you are still in your pj's and slippers. Dress as though you were already on the job. Studies have actually shown that if you look professional, you sound professional.
- It's best not to leave voice mail messages if you can get around it. If you can't, make sure your message is short, sweet, and to the point. (Be prepared to leave such a message BEFORE you call.) If you feel flustered when you get voice mail and suspect that you would ramble on rather clumsily, just hang up.

Online Communication

It is not uncommon today to find yourself communicating with potential employers online using such tools as email, instant messaging, message boards, or virtual job fairs.

When you're using cyberspace to assist in your job search, keep in mind the following guidelines:

- Just because it's in print, doesn't mean that it's true.
- Read the fine lines before agreeing to anything online.
- If you post your resume to a particular job board, know how to un-post in the future.
- Guard your privacy online.
- Answer your job search related emails promptly.
- Never use all capital letters in your email messages. It's equivalent to shouting.
- When sending your resume to an employer, copy and paste it to the end of your email/cover letter message as well as attach the file to the message. Let the employer know that you are doing this, too.

You can't beat the Internet for help in your job search. It's an awesome tool to assist you in:

- researching new duty stations and employment prospects before you even get there
- researching potential employers via their company web pages or search engines
- applying for actual positions via job websites and company web pages
- communicating with potential employers via email, boards, and chats
- keeping in contact with your network contacts and references

Free access is usually available on your military installation through the library or the family services or support centers. It is also usually available at public libraries or copy shops located off the installation. Of course, for a minimal price you can have access in your own home.

If you have a family email account, you may want to consider opening a separate email account just for your job search purposes. This way, an important message won't be accidentally deleted by a family member. Free email accounts are readily available online through such services as Yahoo.com or Email.com. The current service you have may also allow you the option of a separate mail box.

If you haven't used the Internet very much, you need to get onboard quickly. Visit your family services or support center. Many of these organizations offer free computer classes or can point you in the direction of someone on post or base who does. If money isn't an issue, certainly enroll in a basic "how to use the Internet" class through your local education center.

It's easy to hop online and begin surfing. The real challenge is to keep yourself focused on what it is you want to accomplish while you're there. Rather than losing hours on end surfing from interesting link to interesting link, make it a point to obtain a specific amount of information, such as five job leads, and then get offline. Get back online after you've acted on your leads. This will keep your job search efforts moving forward and keep it manageable at the same time.

For a short list of excellent job search websites, refer to the "Red, White, and Blue Pages" at the end of this book.

Your Traditional Job Search Skills: Low-Tech, But High Returns

To give yourself the best shot at being employed, use both high- and low-tech methods simultaneously. It's an unbeatable combination. Such traditional (and sometimes required) tasks as perusing the classified advertisements, attending job fairs, and accurately completing employment applications and forms will go a long way toward helping you achieve your goal.

Classified Advertisements

Even in today's high-tech world, many job seekers will turn first to the classified ads of a newspaper to find out about employment opportunities, but this shouldn't be the only thing you do, and it shouldn't be given top priority in your campaign. Maybe five to ten percent of jobs available are published in the ads. That means you shouldn't devote more than that percentage of your time to them.

Most employers who use the ads run their openings on a particular day of the week. Ads will generally appear everyday, but usually Sundays are the best day to check them out. This can, of course, vary from city to city. Depending upon your location, it wouldn't hurt to quickly check out the openings on a daily basis.

Respond to classified ads immediately in order to get the maximum benefit from them. Once a "perfect" candidate is found, the job may no longer be available even if the ad is still running. Also, it pays to "read between the lines" of each ad before you actually act on it. For example:

The Ad...

Says:	College degree preferred.
Means:	We will consider candidates without a degree.
Says:	College degree required.
Means:	We will not consider you unless you have a degree.
Says:	Get rich quick. No experience necessary.
Means:	I'm a scam and I'd love to have your money.
Says:	Must be able to work independently and have own transportation.

Means:	You'll have minimal support and have to drive your own car.
Says:	Position offered by XYZ Staffing Services.
Means:	You may be the employee of the staffing service rather than the company where you would be working.
Says:	Entry level position.
Means:	You're not going to make much money.

The military lifestyle is full of abbreviations and so are the classified ads. A translation of the more common abbreviations follows:

PC	Personal Computer	**quals**	Qualifications
Yrs	Years	**tech**	Technical or Technician
Min	Minimum	**exp**	Experience
DOE	Depending on experience	**DOQ**	Depending on qualifications
EOE	Equal Opportunity Employment	**M/F/H/V**	Males, Females, Hispanics and Veterans encouraged to apply

Keep in mind the old saying... "If something sounds too good to be true, it usually is." Honest employers use the ads all the time. Some dishonest individuals do the same.

Job Fairs

Job fairs are an excellent way to research employers, network with others, and apply for positions. However, don't expect to walk away from a job fair with a job every time, or you will be disappointed.

When you attend a job fair, you usually emerge with invaluable information upon which you need to act. To reap the most benefit from a job fair, keep in mind that employers participate in job fairs for a number of reasons. They may have positions that need to be filled immediately or in the future. They may attend as a means of advertising their company to others. They may want to give the community the appearance that they are a growing company.

You can make a great impression on potential employers at job fairs by finding out beforehand as much as you possibly can about the companies scheduled to attend. Often, as a means of advertsing the fair, job fair coordinators will publicize a list of companies scheduled to participate. Sometimes, however, they are reluctant to do so for fear that the companies will fill their vacancies prior to the event and cancel their participation. At the very least, try to find out what types of companies will be there, to determine if it is worth your effort to attend.

By obtaining such information, you are able to focus your resume in a given area. You might also consider having a couple versions of your resume prepared which target different areas, if you are able to be flexible. Chapter 6, "Creating An Outstanding Resume," can show you how to focus your resume in a given direction. The following tips will be helpful:

- Have plenty of freshly printed resumes available. Avoid using photocopies.

- You do not need to have cover letters for the job fair.

- Take along your Career History Worksheets from Chapter 2, "Begin at the Beginning." This will save you time in completing employment application forms.

- Select your job fair outfit the night before. You should dress yourself and your attitude as though you were going to the interview itself. (In reality, you're going to a lot of mini interviews.) See Chapter 8, "Interviewing With Ease," for more information.

- Arrive early the day of the job fair. Employers are more likely to listen to you when they haven't already listened to a hundred or so other job seekers.

- Review the job fair map before you start talking to employers. If one isn't provided, do a walk-through and identify all the employers you want to speak with at the event. Make sure the first employer you talk to is one that you are not really interested in at all. This will give you the chance to warm up your communication skills.

- Sell your skills and abilities to employers by using an effective sales sound bite like the one discussed earlier in this chapter.

- Don't be shy. Shyness won't get you a job.

- Use good body language. Smile. Look at people in the eyes. Have a firm, but not bone-crunching, handshake. Let your confidence and sincerity shine through.

- Don't monopolize the employer's time; however, do give the impression that you are a serious contender.

- Take along a notebook or folder. You'll want some place to store the company literature and business cards you collect. You'll also want to make notes after each meeting with an employer. This will help you later when you initiate your follow-up activities.

- Avoid hording all the freebies that are usually available such as pens, pencils, stickers, candy, and notepads. Do take the company prospectus, application forms, and business cards.

- Go to the job fair alone. Leave your spouse and kids at home.

- Avoid eating or drinking at the job fair. Fate will ensure you spill something on yourself or an employer.

Your work really starts AFTER the job fair when you analyze how things went and begin your follow-up calls and letters. The following questions will help you:

- Was attending the job fair worth it?

- Did you generate any potential leads?

- Did you meet any new networking contacts?

- Did you have enough resumes with you?

- Did you effectively communicate with employers?

- Which companies seemed to be most interested in you? Least interested?

- Which companies interested you the most? The least?

- Which companies are you going to send a thank you/follow-up letter and additional resume to within the next couple of days?

Sample Job Fair Follow-Up Letter

Your Name
111 Anywhere Street
Anywhere, Texas 00000
(555) 555-5555
email.address

Date

Company Name
Representative's Name
222 Anywhere Drive
Anywhere, Texas 00000

Dear (Rep's Name Here):

    It was a pleasure meeting you at the recent job fair held at the Fort Bliss, Texas Community Club. It certainly seemed to be a successful event for all concerned.

    During our conversation, you mentioned that your company would be hiring several communication technicians in the near future. I would very much like to be considered for one of those positions. Although I gave you my resume at the time, I am enclosing another one for you which describes my experience in fiber-optics in more detail.

    As a reputable defense contractor, your largest customer is the US military. I am quite familiar with your customer and know, without a doubt, that I can contribute positively to your company. I am a skilled technician and an experienced supervisor. I have over five years experience in the communications field. Additionally, I have held up to a top secret security clearance in past positions.

    I will telephone you with two weeks to answer questions you may have regarding my qualifications. If you would like to contact me sooner, please do so at (555) 555-5555. I look forward to speaking with you in the near future.

Sincerely,

(your signature)

Your Name

Employment Applications

Employers may require that you complete an employment application form in place of, or in addition to, submitting a resume. Employers often use application forms to screen candidates for a given position. Whether or not you get an interview may be decided based upon the content and appearance of your job application. Even though you may have completed ten other applications in one day, treat your eleventh one as though it were the first one you had ever written. Why? Because to the eleventh employer, it is your first one and the impression it makes will be lasting.

Tips for Completing a Job Application

- Obtain the form in advance, if possible. This will give you time to complete a draft and then go final with it using a typewriter. (Yes, they still come in handy once in a while.) If the form is downloadable from the Internet, such as the federal forms off the www.opm.gov website, all the better for you.

- Be prepared to complete the application form at any time. It's not uncommon to show up for an interview and be asked to complete one prior to the actual interview. Having your resume or your career history with you will make your task infinitely less painful.

- Read through the entire form before you begin completing it. Pay special attention to any instructions and fine print. Some employers will use how well you followed directions as a screening tool.

- Don't leave anything blank. If a section doesn't apply to you, indicate it as such with a "N/A" for not applicable.

- Answer the questions honestly. Honestly does not mean, however, negatively. Assume everything you write will be investigated.

- Specify "Position Desired." Always complete this item with a clear answer. If you write "anything" you will get "nothing." Employers want to hire applicants who are focused.

- Avoid leaving any time gaps on the form. If you were unemployed during a certain period, do not write "unemployed" if at all possible. Instead, write down what you were doing during that time (i.e., going to school, raising a family, relocating, or conducting research).

- If asked to describe your work experience in a tiny space, write "Please see the attached resume for a complete answer to this item." If the form specifically advises you not to write "See Resume," then try your best to answer the question as fully as possible under the circumstances. It may even be a good idea to ask a person at the company which way they would prefer you to handle such a situation. Some employers feel that applicants who write "see resume" on the forms instead of directly answering the questions are too lazy to accurately complete the form.

- Be careful about specifying "Salary Requirements." If a question asks you to give your salary requirements, simply write "open" or "negotiable." Writing a specific salary or salary range might result in your application being unfairly eliminated from consideration.

- Consider how to best respond to "Salary History." Employers love to know what you were willing to work for in the past. It gives them an idea of what you may be willing to work for again. It could be that you want to earn much more than you have previously received. You can either honestly complete this type of question or indicate that you "will discuss in person" if you chose. Realize, however, that you may not get that face-to-face meeting because of your answer.

- If you have to use a pen to complete your application and you make an error, simply draw a single line through the error and begin again. If you try to scribble out the error, it will only emphasize the mistake.

- If you feel a question is inappropriate to answer, such as a question about your age, health, or marital status, write "N/A" or "will discuss in person." Some questions are inappropriate and perhaps illegal. You don't have to answer them. An employer will either respect this or not.

- Sign and date the application only after you have carefully proofread it for accuracy and appearance. Be certain you have answered every item.

Application for Employment ——————————————————

General Information

Applicant's Name (Last, First, MI)   _Social Security Number_

Present Address   _Telephone Number_   _Email Address_

Salary Requirements   _Date Available for Work_

Education

School, City, State	Graduate? Yes/No	Degrees Received	Year Attained
High School			
College			
Graduate School			
Other			

Employment History

Last or Present Employer   Supervisor's Name

Address   Telephone Number

Job Title   From   To

Reason for Leaving   Salary Earned

Duties:

Previous Employer   Supervisor's Name

Address   Telephone Number

Job Title   From   To

Reason for Leaving   Salary Earned

Duties:

Previous Employer   Supervisor's Name

Address   Telephone Number

Job Title   From   To

Reason for Leaving   Salary Earned

Duties:

Other Information

What relevant experiences, training, or skills have you had in addition to the above?

Activities you are involved with (exclude organizations which indicate race, religion, color, or national origin of members)

During the past seven years, have you been convicted of a crime, excluding misdemeanors and traffic violations? Yes No (circle answer) If Yes, describe in full.

I certify that the information contained in this application form is true and correct to the best of my knowledge. I understand that any omission or erroneous information is grounds for dismissal if hired. I authorize the references listed above to give you any and all information concerning my previous employment and any pertinent information that may have, personal or otherwise, and release all parties from all liability for any damage that may result from furnishing same to you.

Signature   Date

Your Mindset: Make it So!

You are your most powerful job search tool. It is completely up to you whether or not you become discouraged or maintain an optimistic outlook. It is completely up to you how you handle your job search campaign each step of the way. You can choose to make it an excruciating process that brings you nothing but stress and unhappy thoughts. Or, you can take the healthier approach and realize that this is only one challenge in a life of many to come. Your mindset must be set to the "succeed" button to survive and excel in a job search despite the many distractions that life may present to you in the process. It's all up to you. Make it so!

Your Follow-Up:
It Could Make All the Difference

The difference between a passive job search and a proactive one is follow-up. It is a tool that any job search can't do without and yet so many foolishly do. Without following up on your actions, you risk sacrificing all the hard work you've put into your search. Anyone can throw a resume together, send it out to employers and wait. The end result may be a job or not. Chances are, it will result in the "not." Follow-up can truly make the difference. It's rather like crossing your t's or dotting your i's. It is the finishing touch that better facilitates reaction from employers. How do you do it? Either by mentally or physically noting that you need to contact an employer or their representative again by a certain date to find out the status of your application or just to check in with that person. It doesn't mean you are stalking someone, but it does mean that you are trying to nurture the leads you've already acted upon.

6

Creating an Outstanding Resume

NOTHING STRIKES FEAR in the heart of a job hunter faster than the thought of writing a resume from scratch. Even those who already have a resume may experience anxiety over the thought of having to update or revise it. If you fall into either category, rest assured that you're not alone. Many people feel uncomfortable writing about themselves. It can be difficult to combine your work history into a one-or-two page document. If you completed the Career History worksheets in Chapter 2, "Begin at the Beginning," you are way ahead of the resume writing game. If you haven't completed those yet, you might consider doing so before beginning the work in this chapter.

Why You Need a Resume

Without a well-developed and professional looking resume, your job search is more than likely to suffer at some point. Having a terrific resume will not guarantee you a job either. It can, however, increase your chances of being offered an interview. So, the goal of the resume is simply to get you the interview where, at that point, you can convince the employer into hiring ever so lovable you. In the process, your resume should effectively communicate your skills, abilities, and experiences in such a way that an employer can't wait to meet you face-to-face.

The Truth About Employers

Generally, employers receive more resumes than there are jobs available. Another harsh reality is that they don't always read your literary work of art. If you're lucky, they may spend an average of 20 seconds visually scanning it. They may even leave that task up to a computer or some other equally unappreciative entity. Your goal is to make it past the first cruel cut. To do that, you must tailor your resume in excruciating detail. Sounds like fun, doesn't it? Relax. It won't be so painful if you keep in mind the following truths:

- Your resume is not written for you. It just happens to be about you. It should be written for the employer or the computer that will be scanning it, with focus on the position itself. It is therefore important you know whether a machine or a person reads your resume at the other end.
- There is more than one way to write a focused, well constructed, and winning resume.
- Your resume should be concise, not exceeding two pages in length (unless the employer provides guidance otherwise).
- Your resume should be an effective advertisement of your skills, experiences, and abilities. It should not be a showcase of bland job descriptions or a career obituary.

Creating Your Masterpiece:
A Step-By-Step Blueprint for Success

To create your resume, use the following blueprint. If you have a resume already, still use the guidance and try to look at your product with a fresh eye. You might find yourself totally rewriting after all.

1. Pick the format best suited to the situation.
2. Outline your resume.
3. Draft your resume completely.
4. Edit your resume.
5. Give the resume the acid test.

Pick the Format Best Suited to the Situation

Before you actually develop your resume, decide how it will look when you're finished. It's important to remember that you can have several versions of your resume. What you must do, however, is decide which one will best highlight your features for a given opportunity and focus on this one opportunity at a time.

There are basically three types of resume formats to choose from: chronological, functional/combination and database.

The Chronological Format

Employers typically prefer the chronological resume format, as it allows them an easy look at your work history. Specifically, this format highlights your work experience in chronological order, beginning with your most recent job and working back. Typically, it covers a seven-to-ten-year period. It provides an immediate snapshot of your work experience. See page 83 for an example of a chronological resume outline.

You should consider using this format when:
- you have a consistent work history without any time gaps.
- your experience clearly reflects career progression.
- you are a recent high school or college graduate without an extensive work history.
- you want to stay in your current career field.

You should avoid this format if:
- you want to change career fields.
- you have experience from years and years ago that you want to highlight.
- your resume would reflect time gaps in employment.

The Functional/Combination Format

The functional/combination format is an excellent choice for the military spouse who has had to endure multiple career-disrupting moves. Resumes written in this particular format highlight your skills and abilities more than they highlight your work history. See page 85 for an example of a functional/combination resume outline.

Use this format when:

- you have held a number of jobs.
- you have gaps in employment.
- you want to change career fields.
- you want to highlight skills or experiences from years and years ago.

Avoid this format when:
- you know for a fact that the employer prefers a different format.

The Database Resume

Some companies use sophisticated software to screen resumes and select candidates for interviews. For example, if you are applying for a federal job in Germany you might find yourself writing a Resumix resume. Simply put, this resume must contain certain information in certain places or the resume will be rejected. It also demands that you include certain buzz words in order for your resume to get selected.

Use this format when you know that the company requires it. Meticulously follow any guidance given. Avoid this format when it's not required.

Outline Your Resume

Once you've selected which format to use, outline the resume itself. This doesn't mean start writing about your experiences just yet. Do, however, decide which section components your resume will have. Sections of a resume typically include:

- the heading
- an objective statement
- a summary of your qualifications
- a work history or skills section
- education and training
- professional memberships and awards (if applicable)

Use the sample formats at the end of this chapter to assist you as a good starting point.

Draft Your Resume Completely

By creating your outline first, you have established a framework for your resume. Now all you must do is go back and add the actual information into it. As you do this, it's vital that you avoid critiquing every word or sentence fragment. There will be plenty of time to do this afterward. Draft every section completely regardless of how it reads. Get a rough, finished product in your hands first. Editing will come later. Use the following guidelines to help you create your resume.

The Heading

The heading of your resume lets the employer know your name and how you can be reached. It seems like a simple section, but you would be amazed at how often a phone number or email address is inadvertently omitted. Your heading should contain your:

- full name
- complete mailing address
- area code and telephone and/or fax number
- email address

If you are in between moves, you can list your current and future addresses in a split heading format, if you wish. For example:

Your Name
email.address

Present Address: After July 5th:
111 Current Address   2222 New Address
City, State, Zip   City, State, Zip
(555) 111-1111   (555) 222-2222

There is no need to write "Resume Of" or "Resume" at the top. It's is obvious that it is a resume. Keep your heading simple and uncluttered.

The Objective Statement

An objective statement (for more on this, please see Chapter 2, "Begin At the Beginning") is critical to your resume, whether you physically include it or not. Every line of your document should support a specific objective. It is recommended that you actually put your objective statement on your resume as it will save employers time in trying to figure out what you're all about. There may be occasions, however, when you want to avoid bering locked into an objective statement. Leave it off if you are giving your resume to someone who will pass it on to others for general review. Also, you don't need one if you will be handing the resume out at a job fair. (As an alternative, you could consider a broad-based objective statement for these events.)

A Summary of Qualifications

A summary of qualifications (also called career highlights or career profile) lets the employer decide whether or not he or she really wants to read your resume. Include the following information in your summary (as they relate to the position you want):

- the number of years experience you have.
- any special skills or noteworthy accomplishments you have.
- any particular credentials or licenses you have that are required or impressive.
- one or two value statements about yourself.

A Work History or Skills Section

Here is where the meat of your resume appears. As you draft this section, keep in mind the following tips for describing your experience and skills:

- Don't use full sentences; use descriptive sentence fragments.
- Omit the use of personal pronouns (i.e., I, me, my)
- Quantify your accomplishments.
- Avoid repetitive words and phrases.
- Be consistent with your tense.
- List the most important aspects first.
- Be truthful.

For a chronological resume, include the following in each work descriptive:

- the job title that you held.
- the company's name where you worked.
- the time frame you worked there (use the year to year format – e.g., 1994-2000).
- your experience and accomplishments in that job.

A functional/combination resume is constructed differently from the chronological. Instead of your work history section, you have an Areas of Expertise section with sub-titles highlighting your strongest skills. You also have a Work History section where only your job titles, employers, and time periods of employment appear.

If you are writing an electronic database resume, you could have something totally different depending upon the requirement of the software. Follow the company guidelines carefully. There may or may not be flexibility in this area.

Education and Training

Employers like to know what you know and where you learned it. It's important that you pay close attention to this section. Many people feel inadequate here because they fail to consider training that they've received as education. Learning is learning. If it applies to the position you're seeking, include it on your resume in this section. Obviously, your academic accomplishments, achieved or in-process, should also be reflected here. Keep in mind the following tips:

- If you have an academic degree, spell it out.
  Don't use abbreviations.
  Bachelor of Science Degree, Business and Management, University of Maryland, 2003

- If you have an older degree, omit the year you earned it to avoid dating yourself.
  Masters Degree, International Relations, Oklahoma University

- If you are close to getting your degree, designate yourself as a candidate for graduation.
  Associate of Arts Degree Candidate, Liberal Arts, City Colleges of Chicago, Expected July 2003

- If you do not have a degree, but have taken college courses in the past, combine your education into a single entry.

  Continuing Education, General Studies,
  Troy State University

- If you do not have a college degree or you have not taken any academic post-high school coursework, list any relevant training first in this section. End with your entry showing that you are a high school graduate (if you graduated in the last seven years; otherwise, leave it off). For example:

  Certificate, Senior Supervisor's Training,
  ABC Company, 2003

  Certificate, Equal Opportunity Course for
  Supervisors, ABC Company, 2002

  Certificate, Personnel Technician Techniques,
  XYZ Company, 1998

  Diploma, Tates Creek High School,
  Lexington, Kentucky, 1997

Professional Memberships

If you belong to a professional organization and it fully supports your job objective, list that fact on your resume in an area appropriate for the amount of emphasis you wish to give it.

You should not include the following information on your resume:

- Age
- Height
- Weight
- Marital status
- Salary requirements or history
- Religious or political affiliations
- Health conditions
- References Available Upon Request section (use this only if your resume is short and needs something to balance it out. It's a given that you have references upon request.)

Edit Your Resume

Let's face it. Looks count. Dress your resume for success just as you would dress yourself for an interview. An attractive, professional looking resume stands a better chance than one which is haphazardly thrown together. All the credentials in the world won't help if someone isn't attracted enough to read them. Once you have drafted your resume, take a small break. Get up and walk away from it for a while. Look at it the next day, if necessary. This isn't easy work and a fresh eye is critical for its success. Use the following checklist to assist you.

Resume Checklist

Content:
- ☐ Every line supports your stated (written or not) job objective.
- ☐ Your accomplishments have been effectively quantified.
- ☐ The person reading your resume will be able to understand your terminology.

Layout:
- ☐ Length is one to two pages.
- ☐ Easily readable font is used at 11-12 points (for example, Arial, Century Schoolbook, Times New Roman, Book Antiqua or Bookman Old Style).
- ☐ Upper-and lower-case letters are used rather than all capital letters.
- ☐ Excessive bolding, italics, or bulleting has been avoided (in resumes which will be scanned by a computer, all such formatting should be avoided. It is also possible to use a 10-point font in some situations, thus giving yourself more sell space).
- ☐ Text is not crowded on the page(s).
- ☐ One-inch margins observed on top, bottom, and sides of paper.
- ☐ Quality stationary (including business-sized envelopes) has been used to print out resumes.
- ☐ Spell check and grammar checks have been used by word processing software.
- ☐ An objective, knowledgeable person has reviewed the resume several times for spelling, punctuation, and grammatical errors.

Give the Resume the Acid Test

Now that you've finished your resume, it's time to give it the acid test. Ask yourself one important question:

Does every line on my resume support my objective?

If the answer is yes, kudos to you! If the answer is no, don't despair. A resume is never really finished. It's always a work in progress. You simply need to get to "yes" with the acid test for it to be ready for a given opportunity.

Language and Key Words

The following list of verbs and functional headings can serve as powerful keywords on resumes. Consider incorporating many on your resume.

Powerful Power Verbs for Your Resume

Acted	Budgeted	Created
Adapted	Built	Customized
Addressed	Calculated	Delegated
Administered	Chaired	Demonstrated
Advised	Clarified	Designed
Analyzed	Coach	Developed
Appraised	Collaborated	Devised
Approved	Collected	Diagnosed
Arbitrated	Communicated	Directed
Arranged	Compiled	Dispatched
Assembled	Computed	Drafted
Assessed	Conceptualized	Edited
Assigned	Consolidated	Educated
Assisted	Contracted	Enabled
Attained	Convinced	Encouraged
Audited	Coordinated	Engineered
Authored	Corresponded	Enlisted
Balanced	Counseled	Evaluated

Examined	Lectured	Referred
Executed	Maintained	Rehabilitated
Expanded	Managed	Remodeled
Expedited	Marketed	Repaired
Explained	Mediated	Represented
Extracted	Moderated	Researched
Fabricated	Monitored	Restored
Facilitated	Motivated	Retrieved
Familiarized	Negotiated	Reviewed
Fashioned	Operated	Revitalized
Forecasted	Organized	Scheduled
Formulated	Originated	Screened
Founded	Overhauled	Shaped
Generated	Oversaw	Solved
Guided	Performed	Spearheaded
Identified	Persuaded	Specified
Illustrated	Pioneered	Spoke
Implemented	Planned	Stimulated
Improved	Prepared	Strengthened
Increased	Prioritized	Summarized
Influenced	Processed	Supervised
Informed	Produced	Surveyed
Initiated	Programmed	Systematized
Inspected	Projected	Systemized
Instituted	Promoted	Tabulated
Instructed	Publicized	Trained
Integrated	Purchased	Transformed
Interpreted	Recommended	Translated
Interviewed	Reconciled	Upgraded
Introduced	Recorded	Validated
Invented	Recruited	Wrote
Investigated	Reduced	

Potential Functional Headings

Account Management
Accounting
Acquisition
Administration
Advertising
Analysis and Evaluation
Bookkeeping
Business Management
Career Counseling
Career Development
Client Services
Communications
Community Relations
Community Service
Computer Operations
Computer Programming
Construction
Consulting
Cost Analysis
Counseling
Curriculum Development
Customer Relations
Customer Service
Data Processing
Drafting
Editing
Education
Electronics Engineering
Employee Relations
Environmental Science
Equipment Maintenance
Evaluation
Field Research
Film and Video
Financial Planning
Food Preparation

Forecasting
Fundraising
Graphic Design
Human Services
Inspection
Instruction
Interior Design
Interviewing
Inventory Control
Investigation
Labor Relations
Languages
Legal Assistance
Logistics Management
Management Analysis
Market Research
Marketing
Material Handling
Material Management
Mechanics
Media
Mediation
Merchandising
Negotiation
Nursing
Office Management
Outreach Services
Personnel Administration
Personnel Management
Personnel Supervision
Planning
Plans and Policy
Preventative Maintenance
Product Development
Production
Professional Development

Personnel Management

Personnel Supervision

Planning

Plans and Policy

Preventative Maintenance

Product Development

Production

Professional Development

Program Design

Protective Services

Public Speaking

Publicity

Publishing

Purchasing

Quality Control

Records Management

Recruiting

Reporting

Resource Development

Resource Management

Restaurant Management

Retail

Safety

Sales

Security

Social Work

Staffing

Supervision

Systems Administration

Systems Analysis

Teaching

Technical Writing

Telecommunications

Testing

Training

Vehicle Maintenance

Vehicle Operation

Volunteer Management

Word Processing

Writing

The Adaptable Resume

You're going to be disappointed if you want to have a "one for all" resume. Each opportunity that you apply for will probably differ from the previous one even if they are all in the same career field. The secret to writing your resume is to make it adaptable to different situations. You want to minimize your resume writing, but you certainly want to maximize your chances for an interview. The resumes on page 87-92 illustrate how one resume can be adapted to different formats. You'll never get away from the tweaking of your words, but you can avoid total rewrites every time you apply for a job.

CHRONOLOGICAL RESUME FORMAT WORKSHEET

[Your name, address and contact information.]

_____

_____

_____

_____

Objective
[The objective should reflect the position for which you are applying.]

_____

Professional Summary of Qualifications
[This section should provide relevant highlights of your experience]

_____

_____

_____

Achievements
[Begin with your current job and work backwards.]

_____   _____   _____
(Job Title)   [From]   [To]

_____
[Employer Name]

_____

_____

_____

_____

_____   _____   _____
(Job Title)   [From]   [To]

_____
[Employer Name]

_____

_____

_____

_____

_____   _____   _____
(Job Title)   [From]   [To]

_____
[Employer Name]

_____
_____
_____
_____
_____

_____   _____   _____
(Job Title)   [From]   [To]

_____
[Employer Name]

_____
_____
_____
_____

Education

[Certificate or Diploma], [Course Title], [Sponsor of Course], [Location], [Year Completed]

- _____
- _____
- _____
- _____

FUNCTIONAL/COMBINATION
RESUME FORMAT WORKSHEET

Heading
[Your name, address and telephone number. Do not write the title HEADING on your resume.]

_____

_____

_____

_____

Objective
[The objective should reflect the position for which you are applying.]

Professional Summary of Qualifications
[This section should provide relevant highlights of your experience.]

Areas of Expertise
[Highlight your skills here. See Potential Functional Headings for ideas.]

_____
[Skill Area]

_____
[Skill Area]

_____
[Skill Area]

Name   *Page Two*

[Skill Area]

_____

_____

_____

_____

[Skill Area]

_____

_____

_____

_____

Work History

[Job Title], [Employer Name], [From - To Time Periods OR number of years experience]

-

-

-

-

Education

[Certificate or Diploma], [Course Title], [Sponsor of Course], [Location], [Year Completed]

-

-

-

-

Example of a Chronological Resume BEFORE Editing

Your Name
5555 Street Address
Anytown, Anywhere 00000-0000
(555) 555-5555

**PROFESSIONAL
EXPERIENCE**

October 2001 - Present

PROGRAM RESOURCE SPECIALIST
Army Community Service, Wuerzburg, GE
(0931) 889-7103
Create, design, and coordinate community support groups. Focus groups toward recognized community needs such as Victim Support Group, Adoption Support Group, and Single Parent Support Group. Arrange for media advertisement and provide community awareness booths. Access Family Advocacy Program resources as needed. Utilize Internet and online services for coordination of group activities and updates.

September 1999 -
June 2001

ORGAN TRANSPLANT SOCIAL WORKER
Methodist Specialty and Transplant Hospital
San Antonio, TX 78229
(210) 575-8401
Obtained psychosocial data for assessment of kidney, pancreas and heart transplant patients in pre- and post-outpatient clinics, potential living donors, in-patient hospitalizations for newly transplanted and re-admitted patients. Coordinated home care needs, discharge planning, interdisciplinary collaboration and documentation of assessments and services provided. Facilitated community referrals. Collected data and assisted patients in completing required forms for health care needs. Co-facilitated the Heart Transplant Support Group.

July 1994 -
September 1999

TRANSFER COORDINATOR
Southwest Texas Methodist Hospital
San Antonio, TX 78229
(210) 575-7113
Obtained psychosocial data for assessment and discharge planning. Provided crisis intervention and supportive counseling. Provided community referrals for follow-up care for patients and families. Served on the hospital's Skilled Nursing Unit. Supervised a graduate social work student for one year, by participating in weekly meetings to review progress, assessment analyses, interviewing and basic social work skills. Provided staff development and in-house training with the hospital chaplain on such topics as team building exercises, stress management, anger awareness and management, improving self-esteem, building effective relationships, assertiveness training, problem solving skills, and improving communication skills.

Your Name

July 1992-
July 1994

MEDICAL SOCIAL WORKER
Southwest Texas Methodist Hospital
San Antonio, Texas 78229
(210) 575-4000
Arranged, coordinated, and reviewed discharge planning and coordination of community services for patients hospitalized on the orthopedic, gynecological, and general medicine floors. Completed assessments for psychosocial needs of patients and families. Reviewed and recommended appropriate discharge plans for patients on my caseload at interdisciplinary team meetings. Performed individual and family crisis intervention. Charted daily documentation in patient records. Coordinated transfers to nursing homes. Arranged home care services and provided supportive counseling as needed.

March 1987 -
July 1992

CLINICAL SOCIAL WORKER
Charter Real Hospital
San Antonio, TX 78240
(210) 699-8585
Provided individual, group and family therapy. Obtained bio-psychosocial and needs assessments. Participated as a member of the interdisciplinary team, responsible for weekly documentation and team meetings. Designed community presentations for family and children services in the community. Provided community referrals. Served on the Adult Psychiatry Unit, the Adult Chemical Dependency Unit, and the Adolescent Psychiatry Unit. While serving on the Adolescent Psychiatry Unit for 18 months, provided experiential exercises, educational and resource materials to families of abuse and neglect, reported abuse cases to appropriate authorities, and coordinated support group meetings. Provided individual, group, and family therapy under the supervision of the attending psychiatrist.

EDUCATION
Yeshiva University, Social Work, MA, 1980
Syracuse University, Social Work, BA, 1976
Rockland Community College, Human Services, AAS, 1974

LICENSURE
State of Texas, since 1987 - license number: 014771
State of Florida licensure between 1980 - 1986

VOLUNTEER
Red Cross Volunteer, October 2001 to present
Achieved Trainer status with Army Family Team Building,
January 2002

Example Chronological Resume AFTER Editing

Your Name
5555 Street Address
Anytown, Anywhere 00000-0000
(555) 555-5555

Objective
A position as Community Resource Manager

Summary of Qualifications
Extensive training and experience in the field of community social service. Educationally qualified and maintain current professional license in the State of Texas. Highly skilled facilitator and counselor with in-depth experience in needs assessment, program development, crisis intervention, and referral. Excellent communication, supervisory and administrative skills. Computer literate. Strong attention to detail. Compassionate, caring, and knowledgeable professional. Serve as a volunteer within the community. Willing to work on-call as needed.

Professional Experience

Program Resource Specialist   2001 - Present
Army Community Service, Wuerzburg, Germany

Analyzed survey findings regarding social services needs within a 10,000 plus sized community. Created, designed, and coordinated community Victim, Adoption, and Single Support groups in response to those surveys. Worked closely with installation managers to effectively establish and publicize the programs. Coordinated group activities and updates via the Internet. Evaluated group effectiveness via interviewing techniques and revised as necessary. Arranged for media advertisements through radio, print, and television. Appeared as a subject matter expert on several occasions to successfully market the programs. Participated in community events in various awareness booths. Prepared monthly reports in a timely manner and forwarded to senior management regarding operational status. Additionally, actively participate as a Red Cross volunteer and as a trainer with the Army Family Team Building Program.

Social Worker   1999 - 2001
Methodist Specialty and Transplant Hospital, San Antonio, Texas

Obtained psychosocial data for assessment of kidney, pancreas, and heart transplant patients in pre- and post-outpatient clinics, potential living donors, in-patient hospitalizations for newly transplanted and re-admitted patients. Coordinated home care needs, discharge planning, interdisciplinary collaboration, and documentation of assessments and services provided. Facilitated community referrals based upon in-depth assessments. Collected data and assisted patients in completing required forms for health care needs. Co-facilitated the Heart Transplant Support Group.

Your Name   Page Two

Transfer Coordinator   1994 - 1999
Southwest Texas Methodist Hospital, San Antonio, Texas

As a member of the Skilled Nursing Unit, compiled and recorded psychosocial data for assessment and discharge planning from patients. Provided crisis intervention and supportive counseling on a group and individual basis. Referred patients and families for follow-up care. Supervised a graduate social work student for one year by participating in weekly meetings to review progress, assessment analyses, interviewing, and basic social work skills. Provided staff development and in-house training with the hospital chaplain. Facilitated such topics as team building, stress management, anger management, self-esteem, assertiveness, problem solving, and communication skills.

Medical Social Worker   1992 - 1994
Southwest Texas Methodist Hospital, San Antonio, Texas

Arranged, coordinated, and reviewed discharge planning and coordination of community services for patients hospitalized on the orthopedic, gynecological, and general medicine floors. Assessed patients and families for psychosocial needs. Reviewed and recommended appropriate discharge plans for patients. Participated in interdisciplinary team meetings. Performed individual and family crisis intervention. Charted daily documentation in patient records. Coordinated transfers to nursing homes. Arranged home care services and provided supportive counseling as needed.

Education

- Master of Arts Degree, Social Work, Yeshiva University, New York City, New York
- Bachelor of Arts Degree, Social Work, Syracuse University, Syracuse, New York

Licensure

- State of Texas, License Number 555555, 1987 to Present
- State of Florida, License Number 55555, 1980 - 1986

Example of Same Resume in Functional/Combination Format

Your Name
5555 Street Address
Anytown, Anywhere 00000-0000
(555) 555-5555
email.address

Objective
A position as Community Resource Manager

Summary of Qualifications

Extensive training and experience in the field of community social service. Educationally qualified and maintain current professional license in the State of Texas. Highly skilled facilitator and counselor with in-depth experience in needs assessment, program development, crisis intervention, and referral. Excellent communication, supervisory and administrative skills. Computer literate. Strong attention to detail. Compassionate, caring, and knowledgeable professional. Serve as a volunteer within the community. Willing to work on-call as needed.

Areas of Expertise

Program Management

Analyzed community social services needs surveys findings for a 10,000 plus sized community. Created, designed, and coordinated community Victim, Adoption, and Single Support groups in response to those surveys. Worked closely with installation managers to effectively establish and publicize the programs. Arranged for media advertisements through radio, print, and television. Appeared as a subject matter expert on several occasions to successfully market the programs. Participated in community events in various awareness booths. Coordinated group activities and updates with members via the Internet. Evaluated group effectiveness via interviewing techniques and revised as necessary. Prepared monthly reports in a timely manner and forwarded to senior management regarding operational status.

Personnel Supervision

Supervised a graduate social work student for one year by participating in weekly meetings to review progress, assessment analyses, interviewing, and basic social work skills. Provided staff development and in-house training with the hospital chaplain. Facilitated such topics as team building, stress management, anger management, self-esteem, assertiveness, problem solving, and communication skills. Additionally, actively participated as a Red Cross volunteer and as a trainer with the Army Family Team Building Program.

Clinical Social Work

Obtained and recorded psychosocial data for assessment of patients in a variety of clinical settings. Coordinated home care needs, discharge planning, interdisciplinary collaboration, and documentation of assessments and services provided. Facilitated community referrals and patient follow ups. Collected data and assisted patients in completing required forms for health care needs. Co-facilitated support groups. Provided crisis intervention and supportive counseling on a group, individual, and family basis. Arranged, coordinated, and reviewed

Your Name   Page Two

discharge planning and coordination of community services for patients. Participated in interdisciplinary team meetings.

Program Resource Specialist, Army Community Service, Wuerzburg, Germany,
                    2001 - Present
Medical Social Worker, Southwest Texas Methodist Hospital, San Antonio, Texas,
                    1992 - 1994
Social Worker, Methodist Specialty and Transplant Hospital, San Antonio, Texas,
                    1999 - 2001
Transfer Coordinator, Methodist Specialty and Transplant Hospital, San Antonio, Texas,
                    1994 - 1999

Education

- Master of Arts Degree, Social Work, Yeshiva University, New York City, New York
- Bachelor of Arts Degree, Social Work, Syracuse University, Syracuse, New York

Licensure

- State of Texas, License Number 555555, 1987 to Present
- State of Florida, License Number 55555, 1980 - 1986

7

Job Search Letters
That Mean Business

EFFECTIVE COMMUNICATION skills are the key to being hired in today's job market. Not only do you have to be able to communicate on a face-to-face basis with others about yourself and your qualifications, but you must also be able to communicate effectively on paper and electronically.

Whether it is fair or not, books are often judged by their covers. Similarly, you are often judged by how well you express yourself on paper or via email. You may be the ideal person for the job, but you can forget being hired in a timely fashion unless you can confidently (not arrogantly) communicate your qualifications in writing.

So let's take a closer look at the subject. Here are the kinds of job search letters that you could find yourself writing as you conduct your job search campaign:

- cover letter
- thank you letter
- resume/networking letter

Strategies for creating your letters follow at the end of this chapter.

The Cover Letter

A well-written and organized cover letter is a marvelous job search power tool. The purpose of the cover letter is to introduce your resume to the reader. You should always send one with your resume when you are applying for a job, networking with a contact, or updating your references. It doesn't matter if you are writing your cover letter using a word processor or composing it as an email message. The basic contents are the same:

- heading
- introduction
- supporting body
- conclusion

The Heading

Your heading should include your name, address, telephone number and email address. It should also include a date, the name and address of the recipient, and an appropriate salutation.

1. **Your cover letter, whether hard copy or email, should clearly indicate who you are and how you can be reached.** If you are sending a hard copy cover letter, then the heading of your cover letter should match the heading of your resume. If you are sending it as an email, your return email address will obviously appear on the header, but that's not enough. When you type your name at the bottom of your message, include your address, telephone number, and a repeat of your email address. (Sometimes printed email messages do not show actual addresses, and if your message has been deleted from the computer, it could be a problem.)

2. **Your hard copy cover letter should also include a date.** Be sure to give it in a civilian format. For example, use January 1, 2004 rather than 01 Jan 04. If you've been married to the military for any length of time, you sometimes find yourself using abbreviations for everything. Resist the comfortable temptation to do so in your job search. For email messages, the date will appear in the header automatically.

3. **Your heading on paper should also include the addressee.** You should always address your cover letter to a real person. If you don't know the name of the person you need to send it to, then call the company to get that information. You can always ask the switchboard operator or the secretary for that name. While you are at it, be sure to get the correct spelling of individual's name as well the correct job title. It might require an extra effort on your part, but it will prove well worth the effort. Not only do you get the name of the person you need to contact, but you might also make an additional helpful contact at the company. Managers often rely on the impressions that support staff members get from potential employees. Be sure to be nice to everyone. You never know who may be influential on your behalf.

4. **Fashion your salutation appropriately.** Unless you are personal friends on a first-name basis with each other, stick to a formal salutation. If efforts to uncover a real name are unsuccessful, then use a job title such as Personnel Manager or Human Resources Manager. Stay away from the culturally outdated Sir or Madame or the impersonal To Whom It May Concern.

The Introduction

The introduction of your cover letter should indicate why you are writing the employer in the first place. If you are applying for a specific position, let the reader know how you learned about the vacancy. A traditional opening might read like this:

> *I am applying for the systems administrator position (#55345A) within your company which I read about on Monster.com.*

The traditional approach is professional, but it is not the only way. Sometimes, depending on your career field, it pays to be more creative and dynamic:

> *If you want to hire a sales representative who can aggressively market your quality products and turn an attractive product in a short period of time, then you should hire me today.*

This paragraph is also a good place to name-drop. For example, suppose someone you know suggested that you send your cover letter and resume to a particular employer. If you are sure that the relationship between those individuals is good and the person has given you permission to use his or her name, do so.

Sylvia Young, a former co-worker of yours who now works at the Fort Leonard Wood Army Community Service, suggested that I send you my resume. She thought that you would be interested in my extensive background in social work and how it might be helpful within your Family Advocacy Program.

The Supporting Body

The supporting body of your cover letter should accomplish three important points:

1. It should show the employer that you have the skills necessary to do the job.
2. It should show that you are willing to do the job.
3. It should show that you want to do the job.

It shouldn't, however, be a repeat verbatim of your resume. Here is an example of a supporting body:

As you can see from the attached resume, I have three years of retail sales experience in the electronics industry. Additionally, I have a strong background in personnel supervision, having managed up to five other sales reps at a given time. My organizational skills are excellent and I am highly computer literate. Finally, I am ready, willing, and able to work flexible shifts.

Another way to say the same thing:

You Seek:	I Have:
■ *An experienced sales rep*	■ *Three years of sales experience*
■ *Someone who can supervise*	■ *Experience supervising up to five employees*
■ *Organizational skills*	■ *Excellent organizational skills*
■ *Someone to work flex hours*	■ *Willingness to work flexible hours*

The Conclusion

The conclusion of your cover letter should set the stage for the next step. Leave room for the employer to call you back, but at the same time let him know that you will also follow up yourself within a given time period.

JoAnne Davis
5555 Willow Ridge Circle ■ Columbus, Georgia 55555 ■ (555) 555-5555) ■ jdavis03@email.address

January 15, _____

Medical Forms Plus
Dan Vickers, Human Resource Director
5555 Broad Street, Suite 203
Columbus, Georgia 55555

Dear Mr. Vickers,

Please accept the enclosed resume for consideration for the position of Human Resources Generalist, which was advertised in yesterday's Columbus Ledger.

As you can see from my resume, I have worked in the human resources field for over five years. I have a Master's Degree in Human Resource Management from Boston University and an undergraduate degree in Business and Management from the University of Maryland. For over five years, I have worked as an outplacement specialist with the US Government. In my career, I have had extensive experience in administration, staffing, training, and employee-client counseling. I have also worked in salary administration and employee relations. I am confident in my organizational and communication skills. I am highly motivated and able to work independently or with others on multiple tasks.

The Human Resources Generalist position sounds like the challenge I am seeking. If you find my qualifications equally interesting, I would welcome a telephone call or an email from you.

Thank you in advance for your time and consideration.

Sincerely,

JoAnne Davis

JoAnne Davis

Basic Cover Letter Format

Your Name
City, State, Zip
Telephone
Email

Date

Company Name
Person's Name
Address
City, State, Zip

Dear Name of Person:

Paragraph One: Tell the reader why you are writing in the first place. State whether you are responding as the result of a networking referral, a newspaper advertisement, an Internet posting, or because of your own research.

Paragraph Two: Show the employer how your skills and qualification match those he or she is seeking. If you truly have what the employer is looking for, state it clearly and precisely. If you don't, emphasize what you do have to offer.

Paragraph Three: Close out the letter proactively. Determine the next step for both you and the employer. Restate how you can be contacted and thank the employer for his or her consideration.

Sincerely,

Your Signature

Your Name Typed Here

David Bryan
1111 Southgate Avenue
Havelock, North Carolina 55555
(555) 555-5555
dbryan@email.address

September 1, _____

XYZ Company
John James
1348 Broad Street
Morehead City, North Carolina 55555

Dear Mr. James:

XYZ Company enjoys a highly successful reputation as an aggressive leader in electronic sales. I like that and want to be a contributing member to your team. As stated in Sunday's Morehead City News:

Your Requirements:	*My Qualifications:*
▪ Three years of sales experience	▪ Three years of sales experience
▪ Strong leadership abilities	▪ Supervised up to five sales reps
▪ Administrative skills	▪ Possess clerical and computer skills
▪ Able to work flexible shifts	▪ Able and willing to work flexible shifts

I will contact you the week of September 6th to answer any questions you may have regarding my qualifications. If you wish to contact me before then, call me at (555) 555-5555 or email me at dbryan@email.address. Thank you.

Sincerely,

David Bryan

David Bryan

The Lost Art of Writing
Thank You Letters

If you want to be remembered favorably by an employer, send him a thank you note after your job interview. It only takes a few minutes of your time and it costs only the price of a stamp (or not if you email it). The competitive advantage you could gain from such a simple, common act of courtesy is mind-boggling. Some job seekers neglect to send a thank you note because they don't want to seem too eager for a job or just don't think to do it. This is a mistake.

The thank you letter alone won't get you a job, but it will go a long way to reinforce the good impression that you have already made with someone having influence. You can and should send a thank you letter on the following occasions:

- after you've interviewed for a job
- when someone has given you helpful information
- when you've received a job offer
- after you've been passed over for a job
  (*no* might actually mean *not at this time*)

When you send a thank you letter, you not only show professional courtesy but personal panache as well. Your name will stand out from the other candidates as a result. You create the impression that you would be someone comfortable to work with on a daily basis. Your thank you letter should be short and show a genuine sincerity without overkill. Essentially, a well-written thank you letter gives you the opportunity to do the following:

- Express your sincere thanks for the person's time or advice
- Restate your interest in the position or your specific qualifications for it
- Briefly provide any other information that you may have neglected to give earlier
- Go for broke and *ask* for the job

Basic Thank You Letter Format

Your Name
Address
City, State, Zip
Telephone
Email

Date

Company Name
Person's Name
Address
City, State, Zip

Dear Name of Person:

Paragraph One: Thank the person for her time and consideration. Re-emphasize your interest in the position. If you want the job, say so.

Paragraph Two: Remind the employer that you have the skills necessary to do the job. Your key points should relate to what was discussed during the interview. Mention any relevant points you may have forgotten to say during the interview itself.

Paragraph Three: Restate your sincere appreciation for the interview and your interest in the position. Mention that you are looking forward to hearing from the employer soon.

Sincerely,

Your Signature

Your Name

Carrey Manske
1403-A Churchill Drive
Fort Bragg, North Carolina 55555
(555) 555-5555
cmanske@email.address

April 23, 2005

D & D Consulting Services
Joan David, Personnel Manager
14830 West 14th Street, Suite 131B
Fayetteville, North Carolina 55555

Dear Joan David:

Thank you for your time during our interview on Monday. I enjoyed meeting with you and learning more about the Human Resources Generalist position. I know that I would be strong contributor to your company and I sincerely hope that you will select me for the job.

You mentioned during the interview that you wanted to hire someone who could jump right in and take care of business. My strong organizational, communication, and computer skills could do that for your company.

Again, thank you for the interview and for your serious consideration. I look forward to hearing from you in the near future.

Sincerely,

Carrey Manske

Carrey Manske

Letter Resumes

When you cross a cover letter with a resume, the end result is a letter resume. The letter resume not only introduces you and your intentions to a prospective employer, but it also strives to sell your strongest abilities. It is, in other words, a self-marketing letter. While it shouldn't replace your resume entirely, it can be an effective approach to landing an interview in some situations.

Letter resumes should be written in a direct manner. Let the employer know why you are writing in the first place. Give a summary of your qualifications and mention any noteworthy accomplishments. End the letter with a call for action. Stress your availability for further information. Finally, thank the employer for his or her time.

A letter/networking resume can be used:

- when you want to "test" the waters. You may not know for sure that a position exists, but you want to send out a feeler. You want the employer to learn of your skills and abilities so that you may set the stage for future discussions.
- when you are answering an advertisement and the ad doesn't request resumes.
- when you are networking with someone at a particular company.

Letter resumes should follow the same guidelines as regular cover letters except that you can be more daring and detailed with this type of letter. Your resume letter is your resume and should include your most important selling points. It should seize the reader's interest. The body of the letter should reflect a strong connection between what you have accomplished in the past and what the company you're targeting needs. Company research for this type of letter can't be faked. You need to do your research before writing this type of letter effectively.

Letter Resume Sample

SHARON LEE

151 Springlake Road ▪ Alexandria, VA 55555 ▪ (555) 555-5555 ▪ slee@email.address

March 5, _____

Mr. Jonathan Gilbert
Resource Management Consulting
3535 Main Street
Springfield, VA 55555

Dear Mr. Gilbert:

Customers like to spend their money on products that I sell to them.
If you are interested in hiring a hard-charging sales representative to increase your bottom line, you might be interested to learn about my qualifications.

My Qualifications:

- Bachelor of Science Degree, Marketing, University of Virginia
- Over 10 years of marketing experience involving e-commerce, direct sales, and campaign development and market analysis.
- Strong organizational and communication skills.
- Experienced public speaker.

My Recent Accomplishments:

- Increased divisional pharmaceutical sales by 65% in a large region.
- Created and implemented a successful marketing plan aimed at diverse population.
- Recognized by the American Marketing Association for outstanding work performance.

I am interested in working for your company. If you would like to discuss this proposition further, please call me at (555) 555-5555 or email me at slee@email.address.

I look forward to hearing from you.

Sincerely,

Sharon Lee

Sharon Lee

Job Search Letter and
Email Strategies

- Always proofread your letter to ensure that there are no mis-spelled words.
- Your correspondence should look professional and read easily.
- Be sure that your letter/email and resume work toward the same objective.
- Research employers and the jobs you're applying for.
- Before you write, begin composing your thoughts.
- Emphasize your strengths; don't mention your weaknesses.
- Keep it short. Your letters and emails should not exceed one page.
- On paper, maintain a 1" margin on the top, bottom, and sides of the paper. The heading of your letters should match the heading of your resume. Use the same type of paper for both.
- You can omit the heading on an email message, but it would be prudent to repeat your telephone number and email address at the end of the message, underneath your name.
- If mailing your cover letter, use the same type of paper you use for your resume. Do not repeat your resume line for line in your letters/emails.
- End your correspondence proactively, with a call for action on the reader's part, or with a statement that you will call in the near future.

8

Interviewing With Ease

WHAT DO YOU GET when you cross a terrific resume with an employer who wants to fill a job? If the laws of supply and demand, fate and basic good luck are on your side, the answer is an interview.

Getting to Know You

When you go on an interview, it is a little like going on a blind date. You can't always be sure of what the other person is like. Before the date, you try to find out as much about that individual as you possibly can so that you don't have any nasty surprises. You might even try to establish common ground before your meeting so that you have something to talk about together. In any event, you hope that the two of you will get along well enough to consider a more involved, mutually beneficial relationship.

If you've been on more than one interview before, then you already know that no two interviews are exactly the same. One could last five minutes and another could last for hours. You could interview with one person at a time or with several. The interview might seem structured with the interviewer reading questions off a list, or it might seem so informal that you can't even believe it is an interview in the first place. You might only meet with an employer once before she decides whether or not to hire you, or you might meet with several people several times.

If you feel nervous at the thought of going on an interview, relax. Many employers are just as nervous at the thought of conducting one as you are of going to one. Not all the people who interview are experienced in the interviewing process.

Interview Purposes and Types

There are basically two purposes for the time-honored job interview ritual:

- to get information from an employer about a given career field, position, or company.
- to get hired for a specific position.

Informational Interviews

The obvious goal of this type of interview is to get information and lots of it. This is a great way to interview for a job without interviewing for a job. In addition to gaining the information you want, you are networking with others and getting your name and credentials out there. Your job search will only benefit from effective informational interviews. You can arrange for such a meeting with anyone, including employers, personnel managers, employment agency representatives, or other individuals.

Before you arrange for one, however, do your homework. Ask yourself why you are setting up the interview in the first place. What is your real agenda? Is it to get information about a company, a person, or a particular job? Are you seeking advice or referrals? Perhaps you want to meet someone with decision-making authority so that you can get your resume to him directly. Decide what your reasons are and then develop a list of potential questions that, once answered, will give you the information you want in the first place.

These are the types of questions that you might ask of someone during an informational interview:

- Would you describe a typical workday for yourself?
- How does someone get into your line of work?

- What qualifications are necessary for someone to do your job?
- What are the advancement possibilities?
- What do you like best about your job?
- What do you like least about your job?
- What do you wish you had known about this field before you ever got into it?
- What do you see as being the biggest issues in your business today?
- In what direction do you see this industry going in the future?
- Would you mind glancing over my resume and giving me feedback? I'd like to know if I'm targeting it in the best direction.
- Where would you suggest that I look for more information about this field?
- Can you recommend two other people you know who might be willing to give me more information?

When setting up an informational interview, you should call the person you would like to interview. Ask for a few minutes of that person's time. Explain that you are interested in learning more about their line of work and you would like to arrange a time to meet with them at their convenience. Explain that you would not take more than 20 minutes of their time – and stick to that, unless they indicate otherwise.

When you call to schedule an appointment, you should be prepared to do the interview over the telephone. The person may not be able to work you into his schedule, but he may give you a few minutes of his time right then, over the phone. Have your list of questions ready, along with a pen or pencil, just in case. (This is called telephone scripting. For more telephone tips, refer to Chapter 5, "Job Search Power Tools.")

Another way of arranging an informational interview is to write a letter to the person you wish to interview. This method is more time consuming, but it still works.

Job Interviews

The purpose of a job hiring interview is, of course, to get a job. When you apply for a position and the employer likes your resume or job application, she will generally call you (or have someone else call) to arrange for an interview. It's exciting to get those phone calls. In your excitement, don't forget to obtain the specific information that you will need, such as:

- The day and time that the interview is scheduled.
- Where it will be held (if you are not sure where the company is located, go on a dry run the day before).
- The name(s) of the person(s) who will be interviewing you.
- The name of the person who called you for the interview.
- The name of the company.

Reams of books have been written on the subject of job interviewing. The amount of information out there is positively overwhelming and often contradictory. Interviewing, as stressful as it may be, can be made less stressful by simply preparing beforehand, using common sense and courtesy during the interview, and following up afterwards.

What to Do Before an Interview

You should do several things in preparation for your job interview:

- Gain a real understanding of the company, the position, and the person who will be interviewing you.
- Prepare general answers to basic interview questions.
- Prepare a list of questions you want to ask the employer.
- Put together your interview ensemble, including clothes, accessories, and attitude.

The competition for jobs is tough at all professional levels. One way to gain the edge over other applicants is to learn as much as you possibly can about the company, the position, and the person who will be interviewing you. You can do this by:

- Reading the business pages of the newspaper, trade magazines, or journals.
- Discreetly talking to employees of the company or others who have knowledge of the company.

- Exploring the company's website and reading company literature such as annual reports.
- Researching the company through the Internet and various directories, such as those in the box below.

Useful Resources to Research Companies

- *Dun and Bradstreet's Million Dollar Directory*
- *Standard and Poor's Register of Corporations*
- *Directors and Executives*
- *Moody's Industrial Manual*
- *Thomas' Register of American Manufacturers*
- *Ward's Business Directory*
- *Business Periodicals Index*
- *Reader's Guide to Periodical Literature*
- *Newspaper Index*
- *Wall Street Journal Index*
- *New York Times Index*
- *Bureau of Labor Statistics' Monthly Labor Review*
- *U.S. Global Trade Outlook*

Before you even interview for a particular job, you should have a good idea of what the job might involve and what issues appear to be important to the company. If you can answer these questions about the company before the interview, then you are ready:

- What business is this company actually in?
- What is the biggest challenge facing this company?
- Based upon my limited knowledge, how do I think the company could best handle that challenge?
- What is the reputation of this company and/or the person who will be interviewing me?
- What do I think would be the responsibilities of this job?
- Where might this job fall in the larger organizational picture?

Answering and Asking Interview Questions With Ease

Questions are the very heart of the interview process. Employers ask you questions and you ask employers questions. The key to answering and asking questions with ease is to prepare for them.

When an employer asks you questions about your background, skills, and abilities, you should answer those questions in a way that best highlights your strengths. Simple yes and no or one-line responses don't tell the employer much about you or your capabilities.

Answering questions will be easier if you listen carefully to what the employer is asking. If you are asked a question that you don't know how to answer, ask the interviewer to repeat if. Be truthful in your answers. You don't want to be hired under the pretense of being someone that you're not. That would be an unhappy situation for both you and the employer.

Don't try to memorize answers, either. Know yourself and be relaxed.

Let's take a look at common questions that you may be asked in an interview.

- **Tell me about yourself.** This is a question that employers love. It is so open-ended that your answer often tells the employer everything she ever wanted to know about you and sometimes more than she wanted to know. To answer this question effectively, concentrate on the "work" you. Tell the employer about what you have been doing professionally. Avoid giving your life story at all costs! A good answer to this type of question would be your sales sound bite, a sales pitch that highlights you and your abilities. (See Chapter 5, "Job Search Power Tools," for more information.)

- **What do you know about our company?** If you've done your research, you'll be able to answer this one easily. Learn as much as you possibly can about the employer before you sit in an interview with him. It will give you a competitive edge over others who might not have taken the time to do the same research. At the very least, understand what business the company is in and what their major concerns are in the marketplace.

- **Why do you want to work here?** The employer is trying to figure out your motivation for wanting a job at her company. If this question is asked early, a possible answer might be: "I've heard good things about your company and I was hoping to learn more about it during this interview." If you want to work for that company for a specific work-related reason, say so. For example, "It's a given that Company XYZ is a leader in the banking industry. I like to associate with leaders and I want to be a part of your team. I have no doubt I could bring excellent skills and ideas into your company."

- **Why did you leave your last job?** Be careful how you word your answer to this question. If you were tired of your last job and wanted a change, explain that you felt that you learned and did all that you could in your last position. You just felt that it was time to move on to bigger challenges. Whatever your reasons for leaving, keep your reply positive. The last thing you want to do is sound like you didn't like your last employer. If you left your last job because of your military spouse's transfer, you could simply say that you've recently moved into the area. This doesn't get into why you relocated, just that you did. If you were fired from your last position, explain the situation as positively as you possibly can. Bad-mouthing previous employers, whether they were right or wrong in your dispute, won't score you any points with a potentially new employer. Honesty and sincerity may.

- **What is your greatest weakness?** This is a trick question! The secret to answering this question is to end on a positive note. For example, you might say that you like to see a job through to completion even if it means taking a little more time than you expected. You shouldn't shoot yourself in the foot by saying that you are constantly late to work all the time or you can't stand to work with ignorant people. Let common sense prevail. If you do mention a genuine weakness, be sure you show how you overcame it. By doing that, you show that you are human and you have effective problem-solving skills.

- **What is your greatest strength?** This is an easy one. You'll get more bang from your answer if you answer it in a way that would be meaningful to the employer. For example, if you are applying for a position in the medical field and it is a job that would involve being around patients, you could stress that your people skills are your strength.

- **Tell me about your past accomplishments.** You have them. Be sure you speak about them clearly and concisely when this question is asked. Prepare for this type of question by reviewing your resume before the interview and by reviewing your Career History Worksheets from Chapter 2, "Begin At the Beginning." Tailor your answers to the employer's needs. Show how what you've done in the past can be functionally transferred to enhance his organization.

- **What did you like most and least about your last job?** This is a straightforward question. Again, be careful about presenting any negative information. Think positive thoughts. Speak positive thoughts. Make a positive impression. Your goal is to walk away from that interview with a choice. You can always turn an offer down if you decide that it isn't the right choice for you.

- **Do you prefer working with others or by yourself?** The politically correct answer would be to suggest that you can do both easily. If you have a preference and you know that preference agrees with the job you're applying for, then say so. For example, suppose you are interviewing for a job as a computer programmer. The requirements for this involve sitting alone in front of a computer for most of the workday. If that appeals to you, say so.

- **Why should I hire you?** Don't squirm if you are asked this question. Look the employer straight in the eyes and answer it confidently and completely. Tell him that he should hire you if he wants someone who will work hard. He should hire you if he wants someone who will do a good job and get along with other employees. He should hire you because you are qualified, willing, and ready. He should hire you because you are the best candidate for the position. This is not bragging about yourself. This is reality. If it helps you to get the words out, pretend you are talking about someone else.

- **What salary do you want to earn?** Whatever you say, do not answer this question with a dollar amount. The best approach is to respond with a question, such as "What salary range are you prepared to offer?" If at all possible, get the employer to bring up the numbers first. If you find yourself backed into a corner and you have to answer with a dollar amount, give a salary range rather than one specific amount. Be sure you know what kind of range that should be before you ever step into the interviewer's office. Chapter 9, "Job Offers," can give you more information on salary research and negotiation strategies.

- **How do you spend your spare time?** This is a question that tries to determine who you are personally. Are you a leader in other activities? Are you a risk taker? Will your outside activities interfere with or complement the duties of this job? It is often wise to avoid discussing your political or religious activities when asked this question unless those activities relate directly to the position.

- **What skills do you have that you could put to work for this company?** Again, feel comfortable talking about your skills and abilities. You might want to use a version of your sales pitch here.

- **What qualifies you for this job?** Know the qualifications required for the position and explain how your qualifications match their requirements.

- **What would your last employer say about you?** Regardless of your relationship with your last employer, emphasize something positive. This would also be an excellent time in the interview to offer your reference list.

- **Describe a problem that you had in the past and how you solved it.** The employer is trying to see how you solve your problems. Have one or two good examples prepared for this type of question.

- **Where do you see yourself a year from now? Five years from now?** This is where your ambition is gauged. Answer this question honestly, but again be sensitive to the needs and wants of the employer.

Occasionally an employer will ask you questions designed to shock you or to put you on the spot. Or, if you are being interviewed by more than one person at a time, everyone might try to ask you questions at the same time to see how well you handle pressure. Recognize this tactic if it happens to you and handle it calmly and confidently. If you are being showered with several questions at one time, answer one question at time. Explain that you will answer everyone's question in the order received or in the order of importance.

Potentially Illegal and Discriminatory Questions

Equal Employment Opportunity (EEO) laws and regulations, the Americans With Disabilities Act, and state laws exist to prevent employers from asking you questions that may be discriminatory in nature. Examples of such questions are as follows:

- Do you have any children?
- Do you own or rent your home?
- Do you live alone?
- Do you have a disability?
- What is your religion?
- Whom did you vote for in the last election?
- Are you pregnant?
- Have you ever been arrested?
- Where were you born?
- What is your ethnic background?
- What is your spouse's name and what does he do?

How should you answer such questions? Here you have several choices:

1. You could answer the question point blank even though it is an illegal or discriminatory question.

2. You could get angry and bluntly refuse to answer the question, citing Title VII of the Civil Rights Act in your defense. (Kiss the job good-bye while you're at it.)

3. You could ask the employer to repeat the question and explain how that has anything to do with the position for which you are applying.

4. You could answer the intent of the question, assuming you know what that intent is in the first place. For example, if you are asked if you have children, it is probably because the employer wants to know whether you might miss work often because of your kids. Tell the employer that if this is his concern, he should rest assured that you are a professional and have arrangements in place to handle such circumstances.

Employers often want to know how long you are planning to live in the area if you are married to someone in the military. Again, this is an unfair and potentially illegal question. If you choose to answer that question, indicate that you are planning on living in that community indefinitely. "Indefinitely" can mean anything, and isn't that the way it is when you're married to the military? If you choose to answer that question with a specific time amount, you may or may not be seriously considered for the job as a result. It's not fair, but that's reality. Not all employers feel that way. Some realize that an employee's reasonable longevity should not be an issue. After all, the employer could hire someone who was born and raised in that community only to have that person quit two days after being hired. Keep your interview centered on what you can do for the employer.

Why do employers ask these kinds of irritating questions when it is against the law to do so? For one, they might not know that the questions are illegal or discriminatory. Or, they may not care. An employer who is interviewing candidates for a position usually wants to hire the best qualified person for the job. In their zeal for finding that candidate, these types of questions may just pop out of the interviewer's mouth in one form or another.

In any event, you can't control what is asked of you. You can control, however, your answers. Focus on what you can control.

Questions to Ask Employers

During the interview, you will have an opportunity to ask questions of the employer. Use that time wisely. Be sure you have a list of questions ready for that moment. It's important to remember that you are not the only person being interviewed. You are also interviewing the employer. If you are hired, you may spend more time at work than you do at home. Would you be happy working there? Find out as much as you can about the position and the working environment, so that you can make an intelligent decision if the job is offered to you. Here are some questions you may want to ask during your interview:

- Could you describe what a typical day at work here might be like for me?
- Is this a new position?
- Why did the last person working in this position leave?
- Where does this position fit in the big picture?
- Describe what you feel would be the ideal candidate for this job.
- Who would be my immediate supervisor?
- Do employees like working here? Do they get along well?
- How would my performance be evaluated?
- Is there room for advancement in this company?
- Does the company promote its employees?
- If I were hired and started work this minute, what would be the most pressing issue you would want me to handle?
- What is the normal salary range for such a position?
- What hours would I be expected to work? Would this sometimes include weekends?

Your Interview Ensemble

Don't wait until the day of your interview to get your clothes and accessories together. You'll have more than enough on your mind that day.

Clothes

What should you wear to your interview? You never get a second opportunity to make a first impression. What you wear on an interview may or may not be typical of what you would wear to work every day. So, how can you appear at your best?

- You should wear comfortable clothes that project the image you want to convey.
- Your clothes should be clean and fit you well.
  Try them on before the day of the interview. Make sure all the buttons are where they are supposed to be.
- Make sure you have clean shoes and socks or hose that match your outfit.
- If you are going to wear jewelry, select pieces that won't make unnecessary noise when you move.
- If you are going to wear cologne or perfume, do so very sparingly, if at all.
- Make sure your hair is neatly combed or brushed.
- Don't forget to brush your teeth and wear your deodorant.

Job Search Accessories

Take a pen and something to write on. You may have to fill out a job application form while you're waiting.

- Take your Career History Worksheets with you to help in completing any job application form.

- Take extra original printouts of your resume and your reference list with you in a notebook or briefcase. Be sure you clean out the briefcase beforehand, however. The only items that should be in your notebook or briefcase should relate directly to the interview itself.

The Interview

On the day of the interview, as well as during the interview, you should consider doing the following:

- Go to the interview alone. Do not take your spouse, best friend, or children. Only you are being interviewed.

- Arrive ten minutes early. If you can find a restroom, duck in for one final check.

- In addition to wearing neat and clean clothes, you should also wear a good attitude. Let the potential employer know, by your posture, your actions, and your speech, that you have it together.

- Smile at everyone you meet. Not only is it nature's way of letting your face do aerobics, but it makes people think you are a nice person.

- If you have to wait for a few minutes before the interview, review your resume. Even though you are not yet being interviewed, your behavior is under observation.

- Offer a firm and confident handshake when you first meet with the employer.

- Maintain good eye contact with the interviewer.

- Make sure your body language reflects positive thinking.

- Avoid nervous habits such as tapping your fingers, bouncing your leg, or chewing gum.

- Follow the lead of the employer. Don't try to take charge of the conversation.

- Don't try to fill any moments of silence with forced conversation.

- Listen to what the employer is saying and asking of you.

- If you are offered something to drink, eat, or smoke, politely refuse.

- Answer questions honestly and in a way that highlights your strengths.

- Never say anything bad about your previous employers or co-workers. It will only make you look bad.

- Do not leave the interview without determining the next step in the process.

- Don't be a know-it-all; that is a big turn-off.

- Don't leave the employer with the wrong impression.

- Thank the employer for his time before you leave.

What to Do After an Interview

Take a deep breath and pat yourself on the back. Now it's time to analyze your performance. How did you do? It pays to be objective with yourself here because that is the only way you will improve your interviewing skills. Start by asking yourself these questions:

- How did the interview really go? (Use your gut instincts to answer this one.)

- How did the employer react to me?

- What did I learn about the job, the company, and the person I interviewed with today, that I didn't already know?

- How did people interact with one another at this company? Was I greeted by a friendly receptionist? Did people seem to smile or laugh together?

- Did the employer seem particularly interested in any specific skill or experience of mine? Which one(s)?

- How detailed were the questions I was asked?

- What did the employer think of my resume and cover letter?

- Were all of my questions answered satisfactorily?

- Did I show up on time? Did the employer meet with me on time?

- Did I feel comfortable in the interview outfit I wore?

- Did I maintain good eye contact?

- How could I do better on the next interview?

There are two other important things you should do after your interview:

- **Send a thank you letter to anyone with whom you interviewed.** Besides being both a common and professional courtesy, it is an excellent way to add any information that you may have forgotten to say in the interview itself. Chapter 7, "Job Search Letters That Mean Business," can show you how to write an effective one.

- **Continue your job search.** The temptation to stop and wait to see whether or not you are offered the job is great. Resist it. You must continue your search if you want to be hired. You may or may not be offered that particular job. Don't waste valuable job search time by putting all your efforts into one employer's basket.

Make It a Two-Way Street

The interviewing process is like a two-way street. Employers have a right to know more about you before they hire you. You also have a right to know about your potential employer before you take the plunge. Thoroughly preparing for the interview won't guarantee you the job. It will greatly improve your chances of being hired, though.

9

Negotiating and Evaluating Job Offers

I MAGINE THAT YOU ARE sitting in an interview right this very second. The employer has just offered you a job with an attractive starting salary. Silence hangs in the air as the employer waits for your response. What would you say if you were really in this situation?

Too often, job seekers feel the need to make a decision on the spot. That is not always the best course of action, though. Before you commit yourself to a job and an employer, take the time to evaluate the job offer and negotiate further if necessary.

The process of evaluating and negotiating job offers is one in which job seekers often feel inadequate. Lack of confidence, as a result of poor or no research, coupled with ineffective communication skills and a general lack of timing, contribute to this perceived inadequacy. How can you avoid these feelings and actions of gloom and doom? Arm yourself with good, old-fashioned know-how.

Evaluating the Job Offer

Your hard work will eventually carry you to the point where you are offered a job by an employer. You may be tempted to say "YES!" at the very moment the offer is made. Resist that temptation at all costs. Even if you know beyond a shadow of a doubt that you want that job, bite your tongue. Smile. Smile big if you must. Thank the employer for the generous offer and ask for a couple of days to think about it. The offer will not be withdrawn. On the outside chance that it is withdrawn because you asked for time to think it over, run, don't walk, away from that employer.

Why should you take an extra day or so to ponder an offer? Why not? It's easy to be caught up in the excitement of the moment. An offer, after all, is proof positive of a successful job search. Do yourself a favor and don't accept or decline a job on the spot. Instead, thank the employer for her time and ask her for a couple of days to consider the offer. During that time, weigh the true advantages and disadvantages of that position as it relates to your situation. If it helps, get a second opinion from your spouse or from someone else you trust.

Ultimately, however, the only person who can honestly decide whether or not an offer is the right one for you is you. Your decision should be based upon your needs and your wants. The following evaluation checklist offers valuable points of consideration.

Job Offer Evaluation Checklist

Yes	No	Consideration
❏	❏	Do I fully understand what would be expected of me?
❏	❏	Do I feel that my skills and abilities match the work to be done?
❏	❏	Does this job support, directly or indirectly, my career goals?
❏	❏	Does the company have a good reputation?

Y   N

☐   ☐   Does the company offer room for advancement?

☐   ☐   Can this job move with me if my family is transferred?

☐   ☐   Did I meet the person who would supervise me?

☐   ☐   Did I get a good feeling about this person?

☐   ☐   Would our work styles complement one another?

☐   ☐   Did I like the work environment itself?

☐   ☐   Are the working hours acceptable to me and my lifestyle?

☐   ☐   Would I be required to work overtime?

☐   ☐   Will I be required to travel?

☐   ☐   Did the employees working there seem to be happy?

☐   ☐   Is there a low turnover rate of employees at this company?

☐   ☐   Would my performance be fairly evaluated on a periodic basis?

☐   ☐   Does the company offer training and/or continuing education opportunities?

☐   ☐   Am I satisfied with the total compensation package?

As you evaluate your job offers, remember that the perfect job does not exist. The challenge is to find one that has more advantages than disadvantages. Once you make your decision, don't look back. You can't change the past but you can affect the future.

Negotiation Basics

You do not have to accept the initial offer made to you by an employer, unless you are completely satisfied with the contents of that offer. You can always negotiate for a better one.

What can be negotiated? Certainly, everyone knows that you can haggle over a salary. Salary, however, is just one part of the compensation picture. You can also negotiate benefits as well as work content. In fact, benefits often represent up to 40% of a total compensation package.

Learning or reviewing effective negotiating techniques will increase your chances of being fairly compensated. You can use these techniques when you are in the middle of negotiating a job offer or you can use them when you want to ask for a raise.

Salary

"Money doesn't make the world go around, but it sure helps."
– **Unknown**

Would you accept the first salary offered to you by an employer? What if you were asked to name your salary? How would you answer that loaded question?

Let's be honest. Just about everyone who works for a living likes to bring home a paycheck. Almost everyone would agree that the bigger that check is, the better. Like it or not, it is through our paychecks that society unwittingly keeps score on our value at work. Is that fair? No, but it is reality. You must remember that your pay doesn't reflect your true value in life. It is simply one point of several points to discuss in the employment process.

Be certain it is a point of discussion that you don't bring up first in the negotiation process. He who has the gold makes the rules, right? He who has the job to offer should be the first person to mention anything about salary or benefits. This point may come up in the first interview or in later interviews. In any event, let the employer bring up the issue first.

Keep in mind, there may or may not be room for an employer to negotiate with you. Perhaps the salary was advertised along with the job announcement and that is that. The employer may honestly not have any flexibility about what he can offer you financially. You will never know until you ask, though. If you are uncomfortable or shy about discussing this issue, you should try to get over it. You are not asking anyone for any favors. You are trying to be fairly compensated for your skills and abilities. Negotiate as an equal.

The salary that you accept more often that not becomes the basis for your future salaries. It stands to reason, then, that you should determine what you want to make before you ever get to that point in the interview process. One way to determine your salary range is to research current compensation levels. In other words, what is everyone else making for doing the same job? You can do that through a number of resources, including:

- Nationally published annual salary surveys.

- State departments of labor salary surveys.

- Published private sector pay scales.

- The classified advertisements (sometimes salaries are listed with ads).

- The business pages of the newspaper.

- Books such as the Department of Labor's *Occupational Outlook Handbook, Jobs Rated Almanac, American Almanac of Jobs and Salaries,* and *American Wages and Salaries Survey.*

- People whom you know personally or professionally who may be willing to discuss this often sensitive issue.

In determining your salary range, realize that pay will fluctuate from location to location. The cost of living and therefore the salary structure are significantly different between the communities of Sierra Vista, Arizona, and Washington, DC.

The flexibility that an employer has regarding the salary that he offers you will have a lot to do with the size of the company and its financial situation. Larger companies are more apt to have a set salary structure in place than smaller companies where you might be required to do a variety of duties. Smaller companies, on the other hand, may not have much flexibility with salary offerings.

You will always want to understand how the employer plans to pay you, should you accept his offer. For example, you might have a pay structure that is a straight salaried position. You might receive cash allowances or performance bonuses in addition to that salary. The pay offered might not be a salary at all. It might be a strictly commission-only position, meaning that you earn a percentage of what you sell. If you have a bad day and don't sell anything, then you don't earn any money that day. The job might even pay a salary and a commission. The salary or pay structure for a given position will be affected by the type of position, the company, and the regional going rates for similar positions.

You should be able to express your salary requirements in solid terms. How much do you want to make a year? A month? A week? An hour? A minute? To calculate a salary into smaller amounts, do the following:

Annual Salary / 12 months	=	Monthly Salary
Annual Salary / 51 weeks	=	Weekly Salary
Weekly Salary / 5 days	=	Daily Salary
Daily Salary / 8 hours	=	Hourly Salary
Hourly Salary / 60 minutes	=	Per Minute Salary

Take, for example, a job offer at $18,500 a year. This equals:

18,500 / 12	=	1541.67 monthly
18,500 / 51	=	362.75 weekly
362.75 / 5	=	72.55 daily
72.55 / 8	=	9.07 hour
9.07 / 60	=	.15 per minute

Don't forget that these figures represent your potential pre-tax pay, not your take-home pay.

After you've researched the going rates, look at your own financial situation. How much income do you need? By looking at your current income, expenses, assets and liabilities you can get a feel for what you realistically should strive to earn. Do not let your current financial situation be the sole factor for determining your salary range. Never discuss your personal financial needs with an employer during the negotiation process. Keep the subject centered professionally on fair compensation for your skills and abilities.

Hourly Wages:

Classified as nonexempt employment. This means that an employee is paid for work by the hour. Overtime is paid at a rate of time and a half for hours worked during the labor week over 40 hours. Nonexempt employees are covered by the Fair Labor Standards Act.

Salaried Employment:

Classified as exempt employment. This means that an employee works for a straight salary and does not get paid for overtime. Exempt employees are not covered by the Fair Labor Standards Act.

Hourly	Weekly	Monthly	Annually
5.00	200.00	866.67	10,400.00
5.50	220.00	953.33	11,440.00
6.00	240.00	1,040.00	12,480.00
6.50	260.00	1,126.67	13,520.00
7.00	280.00	1,213.33	14,560.00
7.50	300.00	1,300.00	15,600.00
8.00	320.00	1,386.67	16,640.00
8.50	340.00	1,473.33	17,680.00
9.00	360.00	1,560.00	18,720.00
9.50	380.00	1,646.67	19,760.00
10.00	400.00	1,733.33	20,800.00
10.50	420.00	1,820.00	21,840.00
11.00	440.00	1,906.67	22,880.00
11.50	460.00	1,993.33	23,920.00
12.00	480.00	2,080.00	24,960.00
12.50	500.00	2,166.67	26,000.00
13.00	520.00	2,253.33	27,040.00
13.50	540.00	2,340.00	28,080.00
14.00	560.00	2,426.67	29,120.00
14.50	580.00	2,513.33	30,160.00
15.00	600.00	2,600.00	31,200.00

Hourly	Weekly	Monthly	Annually
15.50	620.00	2,686.67	32,240.00
16.00	640.00	2,773.33	33,280.00
16.50	660.00	2,860.00	34,320.00
17.00	680.00	2,946.67	35,360.00
17.50	700.00	3,033.33	36,400.00
18.00	720.00	3,120.00	37,440.00
18.50	740.00	3,206.67	38,480.00
19.00	760.00	3,293.33	39,520.00
19.50	780.00	3,380.00	40,560.00
20.00	800.00	3,466.67	41,600.00
20.50	820.00	3,553.33	42,640.00
21.00	840.00	3,640.00	43,680.00
21.50	860.00	3,726.67	44,720.00
22.00	880.00	3,813.33	45,760.00
22.50	900.00	3,900.00	46,800.00
23.00	920.00	3,986.67	47,840.00
23.50	940.00	4,073.33	48,880.00
24.00	960.00	4,160.00	49,920.00
24.50	980.00	4,246.67	50,960.00
25.00	1,000.00	4,333.33	52,000.00
30.00	1,200.00	5,200.00	62,400.00
40.00	1,600.00	6,933.33	83,200.00
50.00	2,000.00	8,666.67	104,000.00

Salary History

Companies will often ask you to supply them with a salary history before they agree to interview you for a given position. They do this so that if they decide to offer you a position, they can base your future salary on your past earning history. This isn't always fair. If an employer asks for a salary history, however, provide it. Here's an example of how you might best present your salary history:

Jane Baker
1285 Jamestown Road
Spanaway, WA 55555
(555) 555-5555
janebaker@internet.com

Salary History

Title	Company	Hourly	Time Period
Representative	University of Maryland	13.50	2003-Present
Office Manager	Department of Defense	12.75	2000-2003
Data Entry Clerk	Temps Plus Agency	10.25	1999-2000
Receptionist	D&B Advertising Agency	9.50	1998-1999
Sales Associate	Cable TV Today	9.00	1997-1998

Benefits

Pay is only one part of the compensation package. You may be offered benefits as well. Benefits can often represent up to 40% of your total compensation package, and should be negotiated if possible. If you have been offered a job and there has been no mention of a benefits package, ask the employer about them. You should, however, negotiate your salary separately from any benefits offered to you.

Examples of benefits which an employer may offer include:

- worker's compensation
- unemployment compensation
- Social Security
- child and elder care
- severance package
- lunch and rest breaks
- medical
- dental
- vision
- pension plans
- holidays and vacations
- sick leave
- funeral and bereavement time off
- performance and bonuses
- company stock plans
- profit sharing
- pre-tax annuities with matching company contributions
- life insurance
- disability insurance
- loan guarantees
- personal days off
- educational assistance
- automobile or mileage
- club memberships and discounts
- credit cards

Work Schedules, Locations, and Contents

In addition to salary and benefits, you might be able to negotiate your work schedule, the location of your job, and the actual content of it.

Work Schedules

There are a number of different work schedules in existence today. An employer may or may not be able to negotiate with you on this, but it's worth a shot if it is an issue of importance to you. The actual hours and days that you will be required to work will depend upon the type of business that the company does. Here are some employment schedules to consider:

- Full-time – work 40 hours or more a week.

- Part-time – work 39 hours or less a week.

- Job share – share the position with another employee.

- Contract – work on a specific project for a given length of time.

- Flex-time – work your own hours as long as the job gets done.

Locations

Depending upon the type of business involved, you might be able to negotiate where you work. Alternatives to consider:

- Work at the company itself.

- Work at a branch of the company that is more convenient to where you live.

- Telecommute from your home.

Strategies That Work

Effective salary negotiators use several strategies that result in salary offers that best reflect their value. These include:

- Know what you want in a salary before the subject comes up and know that your skills and abilities are worth every penny of it.

- Do not accept a position until you are satisfied with the salary offered to you.

- Let the employer be the one to bring up the subject of compensation first.

- If you are asked what salary you want to earn, deflect the question back to the employer. Try to get him to state a range or an amount first. "What are you prepared to offer?"

- If you must state a figure, ask for 10-15% more than you really want. You can negotiate down much easier to a satisfactory salary than you can up to one that pleases you.

- Be confident in your speech, your appearance, and your actions. If you are perceived to be someone who should be paid more, chances are that you will be offered more.

- Be able to back up why you want more money. You have to give solid examples of why you should be paid more.

- Offer solutions to the employer. If you ask for something and you cannot get it, ask why. Once you know why, then you can offer an alternative course of action. Work with the employer, not against him.

- If you don't like the offer made to you, don't get angry. Anger will only work against you. Instead, establish the duties of the position again. "Let me see if I understand the duties of this position fully . . ." By doing this, you remind the employer of the amount of work involved and you can then suggest a higher salary for that amount of responsibility.

- If you are still not offered a salary that is acceptable to you, define your first raise. "I would accept that salary, but only if I would be given a raise within six months to this salary."

- Get it in writing. If the employer will not provide you with an offer letter or an employment contract, design your own and have the employer sign it. Your contract should at least include your job title, description of duties, starting salary, benefits, and terms of employment.

When You Don't Get Offered a Job

"No" is a word you will probably hear regardless of how qualified you may be for a position. Do not take this personally. Instead, ask the employer why you were not selected. You might be pleasantly surprised to learn that even though you did everything right, the company just decided to hire from within. Maybe they decided not to hire anyone at all. You might also find out that you were over- or under-qualified for the position. Perhaps the person who interviewed you felt that your style and the company's style were not compatible. There could be any number of reasons why you were not selected. You should try your best to find why you were not chosen. If the reason ends up being something that you can improve upon for future interviews, do so.

Becoming Fit

Negotiating and evaluating job offers represent an important part of your job search activities. You should feel comfortable and totally confident in this area. Remember that you are striving for a mutually beneficial "fit." If a fit is possible, great. If a fit doesn't seem to be possible, accept that and go on to your next opportunity.

10

Managing Your Own Career

THERE WAS A TIME when you could depend upon your employer to manage your career for you. It was understood that if you worked hard, you would be rewarded somehow. It was a given that your employer would help you to gain additional skills. Today, that is not true. While some employers still provide excellent advancement and training capabilities, many expect you to take care of your own needs. The sooner you accept that new job search fact of life, the better. The laws of the employment jungle have changed because the jungle itself has changed. Those who follow the old rules are sure to fall by the wayside or, even worse, stay in the same place for the rest of their careers.

On Your Own

Today, the only person upon whom you can truly depend is yourself. You are the person most concerned about yourself and your job or your career. If this thought terrifies you, relax. You're not alone. You can learn how to manage your own career.

One way to do this is to think of yourself as an independent company. On one hand, you are the president of that company. It's your job to oversee your organization. You must think about your present, but you must also plan for your future. On the other hand, you are your company's best customer. As such, you are always right and you deserve first class service.

There's no denying that balancing a job or a career with a life married to the military is tough. Rather than look upon that life as an obstacle, look at it as an opportunity. What can you gain from your lifestyle? What edge can you have over others who don't share the same experiences as you? Keep yourself focused on your own interests. Focus, as we have seen throughout this book, is necessary. Focus means channeling your efforts and thoughts into a specific direction. When applied to your job search, it means:

Formulating a full circle job search plan.

Overcoming any weaknesses by concentrating on your strengths.

Choosing to take responsibility for your own employment situation.

Using and developing your existing network of resources.

Succeeding according to your own standards.

Focus is necessary in order to manage your own career. If it helps, begin managing your career by visualizing the end of it. Where do you ultimately want be professionally? Imagine that you have all the training, certifications, or degrees that you would ever need. Poof. They're yours and you've used them for years. Now, what is your job? As a step further in this visualization process, draft a resume for that job which will become a path for you to follow. You can achieve anything you want to achieve if you want it badly enough. Think it. Believe it. Do it.

Creating Your Own Advancement

The idea of advancement is a lot like the idea of success. Everyone has their own definition of what it means to them. There is no right or wrong answer. There is only your answer. The challenge lies not in defining advancement but in making it happen. The following guidelines can help you meet that challenge:

- Understand the difference between job titles and power. People having menial sounding job titles often carry more weight than those having impressive sounding ones. Snub someone because you think that their role is not important and you might find that you have just snubbed yourself.

- Listen.

- Find a mentor. Not only will you flatter someone and make an important networking contact, but you might also learn something.

- Be a mentor. When you empower another person, you really empower yourself. People who try to keep information all to themselves in order to be more powerful on the job are actually stupid, insecure, and often ineffective.

- Avoid associating with stupid, insecure, and ineffective people.

- Associate with positive people.

- Keep your resume and your skills updated.

- Keep your options open. Never make a decision one way or the other until you consider it and its implications fully.

- Be willing to take calculated risks. An old expression says it nicely: *A ship in the harbor is safe, but ships were built to weather storms and travel the world... not hide in calm waters.*

- Review your goals periodically and revise them as necessary.

- Think big.

- Think really big.

- Dress your attitude and yourself up at least one professional level above where you currently exist.

- Rise above personality differences with someone by concentrating on the tasks to be accomplished rather than on how much you can't stand that person.

- Be friendly to your co-workers, but maintain a respectable distance.

- Be honest but firm in your speech and actions.

- Be a team player and a team cheerleader.

- If you don't understand something, ask. It's better to sound like a fool than to actually be one.

- Leave any personal problems you have at home. Likewise, leave your work problems at work. Scarlet was right. Tomorrow will be another day and the work problems will still be there in the morning.

- Think like a sponge. Absorb all the knowledge around you and mentally file it away for use or reference at a later date.

- Make things work better.

- Do more than is required of you.

- Join a professional association that is active in your area.

- Be the person that people turn to when they have work-related problems.

- Make mistakes. A life without them is a life without learning.

- Read everything you can get your hands on about your job, career field, and the company that hired you or might hire you.

When You Decide to Leave a Job

The latest statistics indicate that the average person will change jobs at least five times in the course of a lifetime. Working military spouses can expect to change jobs even more than that. For a spouse married to someone over a 20-year period, that can possibly amount to seven different jobs reflecting seven different moves . . . and that is being generous to say the least.

Obviously relocation due to a spouse's military transfer is one reason you might decide to leave a job. There are other reasons as well. Perhaps you find that you don't enjoy the work. Over a period of time, almost any job can seem to become routine and dull. Maybe you are offered a position that pays more. The prospect of making more money is always an enticement to leaving a job, whether you like the one you have or not. Maybe you decide to leave because of changes occurring within the company itself. Perhaps you are not satisfied with a new manager's way of doing business. Perhaps you are fired. Maybe you just want a change of pace.

The reasons for leaving a job can obviously vary. Whenever and for whatever reason you decide to leave, do yourself a BIG favor. Leave gracefully, tactfully, and with as much professionalism as you can possibly muster, regardless of the situation. You can bet that you will always be remembered for how you left a job by those left behind.

- Give at least a two-week notice if at all possible. If you are able to give more of a notice, do so.

- Don't leave in haste or anger. Even if you can't stand the job or the people you have worked with, let them know that you have appreciated the experience.

- If you are being fired and you don't understand why, seek clarification and base any further actions upon the facts.

- Be confident in your decision and stick to it.

- Don't burn the bridges behind you. You may have to cross back over one day.

- Don't quit giving your job your best effort just because you're leaving. You will be remembered in a less than favorable way if you do.

- Find out what you have to do to leave the company and do it. You might have to write a letter of resignation or go through the human resources department to "out process."

- Tie up any loose ends on the job. Write out detailed notes for your replacement if necessary.

- Give the company a forwarding address.

- Obtain references, complete with addresses and contact numbers, for future use before you leave.

- Make it a point to keep in contact with your references from that company after you're gone.

- If at all possible, have another job waiting for you.

- If having another job waiting for you isn't possible or feasible, at least conduct some research on future potential employers.

- Accept and manage any stress you might feel from leaving a job, whether you're happy to leave it or not.

When You Decide to Leave the Military Lifestyle

How many times have you heard, "when we retire..." or "when we get out..."? Maybe you have even caught yourself saying it. The truth is, sooner or later everyone leaves the active duty military lifestyle. Either your spouse retires after many years or perhaps he or she decides to leave after a couple of years. Regardless of your situation, the transition from the military is not always as easy as you think it would be. Life, as we often know it in the military or married to it, is very cut and dry. It isn't always fair (surprise, surprise). Often, it seems as though there is nothing we can do about that unfairness. Sometimes you have to endure and know that things will get better.

Leaving that world can be traumatic, even if you have waited for that moment for what seems like forever. Imagine going to a store and not having to show an ID card to get in to shop. Imagine life without a main gate or a community of transient friends. Imagine staying in one community for a very, very long time. Imagine living in one house forever where you can plant trees in the yard and eventually see them grow up without having to wonder what they would look like from the other side of the world. You have always known that a world existed without the military influence, but you may have not experienced that world for quite some time.

When that transition comes, ease into it as best as possible. The road may be bumpy at first. Understand that the transition process is not "easy street" and deal with it just as you have dealt with other challenges of being married to the military lifestyle.

Career-wise, transitioning from the military can represent a wonderful opportunity for you. How many times have you heard married service members jokingly say that when they retire or separate from the service, they were going to follow their spouses around the world for a change? All kidding aside, if you have made career sacrifices for your spouse, now he or she can make them for you.

To make your transition easier, take full advantage of all of the resources available to you on the installation where you are stationed, such as the Transition Assistance Programs, Job Assistance Centers, and the spouse employment programs offered at the Family Services Centers, Family Support Centers, Work-Life Programs or the Army Community Service Centers. (These programs are discussed in detail in Chapter 3, "Planning for Success.")

Additionally, private military-related organizations also offer career guidance and support to transitioning service members and their spouses, usually for the price of membership in their organizations.

Having a Successful Career

Having a successful career is certainly within your reach. If you already have one, continued success is possible. Achieving that level of success, as you individually define it, is possible.

- Follow your gut instincts. An opportunity may look good, smell good, and seem good, but if it doesn't feel good to you, pass it up.

- Don't be afraid to change career directions. You might be the best at what you do, but if you are tired of doing it, your work will suffer, the people you work with will suffer, and you will suffer. Have the courage to realize when it's time to move on and do it. Periodic self-assessments can help you to consider alternatives and make appropriate decisions.

- If you work in a profession that relies on state certifications and you want to stay in your profession, plan ahead as best as possible. Find out what is required for you to practice in other locations where you might relocate. You may or may not be able to stay in your exact profession if you choose to relocate with your military spouse. Get all the facts and make a decision that is right for you and your situation.

- Continually nurture and add to your network. People are the greatest resources ever and the more whom you know, the greater your connectivity. Don't just take from your network, give as well. It's that give and take action which strengthens your network in the first place.

- Keep abreast of current job search strategies. This will make you less vulnerable in the event you must look for a job without warning or in the event you relocate with your spouse.

- Keep yourself up-to-date on the events happening within your company. It will help you be a stronger contributor to your organization, and it will help you to better manage your career should you want to move up or out in the future.

- Accept responsibility for your own actions.

- Look to the future but don't make the mistake of ignoring the present.

- Maintain or get a sense of humor.

- Plan your career around a job that you love doing.

Married, Mobile, and Motivated: It's Not a Myth

You can be married to the military, mobile, and motivated for the new job market all at the same time. It might be a bit of a balancing act, but then isn't that all life is in the first place? If you feel that this book has provided you with practical job search advice, then my goal has been met. In the end, however, you must decide how you will handle your job search and your career. You have two basic choices. You can take the proactive path. Go out there and give it your best shot. Don't be afraid of failing because in failing you learn and therefore succeed. Or you can be reactive and let the world happen around you. Take what is offered to you (if anything is offered) and be content. The choice is purely yours. If you have this book in your hands, then I suspect that you have made the decision to be proactive. Kudos to you. You obviously understand that something must give in order to gain something else. That "something" is different to everyone. To you it might mean making the decision to stay in one location to advance with your job while your spouse transfers to a new assignment. To others, it might mean making the best of a mobile situation. Whatever your choice, be confident in it. If you find yourself professionally stalled, refer back to the basics.

There is an old saying in the military that the best place to be stationed is the place that you just left or the one that you might be going to . . . never the one where you are stationed. That doesn't have to be true. Life, as well as your career, is what you make it. Ralph Waldo Emerson once suggested that we handle life (and perhaps our career?) by finding a star and hitching our wagon to it. Whether you have hitched your wagon to a star, a bar, a stripe, or a bird . . . enjoy the ride. You only live once. If you choose to work or have a career somewhere in between the moves, the kids, and the general chaos . . . all the better for you and for the lives you are sure to touch along the way.

Red, White, and Blue Family Centers
Useful Contacts for Job-Seeking Spouses

Family Centers can serve as an excellent starting point in your job search, whether you are new to a particular installation or not. They can assist you in preparing your resume and planning your job search campaign. They are able to help you locate job opportunities on and off the military installation you call home. To locate the one nearest you, access the following website:

<u>www.dmdc.osd.mil</u>

This is the Defense Manpower Data Center's homepage. It is a world-wide relocation tool for use by military service members and their families. Once you are here, select DoD Community. Login using your SSN/ID, birthdate, and last name. (Use of the site is restricted to active duty service members and their families). Select Activity Locators and then SITES (Standardized Installation Topic Exchange Service). Login once again using your SSN/ID, birthdate, and last name. At that point, select your installation of interest and the "Support Services" option once you're viewing individual installation information. Depending upon your branch of service, the family center will be listed as the family center, the family support center, or the Army Community Service. Current contact information should be available for you at this point. This is an outstanding website as it also provides you with tons of information about your military community and the world located right outside the front gate.

Several other websites specialize in providing career transition assistance to military personnel. Some of them also include employment information for military spouses. Periodically check out these sites for such information:

Army Career and Alumni: www.acap.army.mil
Corporate Gray Online: www.greentogray.com
Department of Defense Transition: www.dodtransporal.org
Military Spouse Resource Center: http://militaryspouse.org
e-Vets   www.dol.gov/elaws/
                                   evets.htm

Red, White, and Blue Pages

Online Resources

Career Research

America's Career InfoNet	www.acinet.org/acinet
Career Guide to Industries	www.bls.gov/oco/cg
Hoovers Online	www.hoovers.com
Occupational Outlook Handbook	www.bls.gov/oco
The Riley Guide	www.rileyguide.com
Wall Street Journal Job Services	www.careerjournal.com

Education Related

The Wired Scholar	www.wiredscholar.com
CollegeNet	www.collegenet.com
Dept. of Education Financial Assistance	www.ed.gov/finaid.html
Peterson's	www.petersons.com

Government Links

The following websites will lead you to listings of job opportunities (or to organizational web pages which have links to job listings) within the Federal Government.

Army Civilian Personnel Online (CPO)	www.cpol.army.mil
Civilian Human Resource Management Agency	www.chrma.hqusareur.army.mil
Defense Commissary Agency (DeCA)	www.commissaries.com
Defense Contract Audit (DCAA) Agency Service	www.dcaa.mil
Defense Finance and Accounting	www.dfas.mil
Defense Information Agency (DISA)	www.disa.mil
Defense Intelligence Agency (DIA)	www.dia.mil
Defense Logistics Agency (DLA)	www.hr.dla.mil
Department of Labor	www.dol.gov

Federal Aviation Administration (FAA)	www.faa.gov
Federal Bureau of Prisons (BOP)	www.bop.gov
FedWorld	www.fedworld.gov
National Aeronautics and	
Space Administration	www.huminfo.arc.nasa.gov
National Institutes of Health (NIH)	www.jobs.nih.gov
U.S. Postal Service	www.usps.com/
	employment
U.S. Public Health Service	www.usphs.gov
U.S. State Department	www.foreignservice
	careers.gov
USA Jobs	www.usajobs.opm.gov

Major Employment Websites

America's Job Bank	www.ajb.dni.us
American Jobs	www.americanjobs.com
Best Jobs USA	www.bestjobsusa.com
CAREERspan	www.careerspan.com
Career Builder Network	www.careerbuilder.com
Career Cast	www.careercast.com
Career Hunters	www.careerhunters.com
Career Magazine	www.careermag.com
Career Mart	www.careermart.com
Career.com	www.career.com
Careers 2000	www.careers2000.net
Career Shop	www.careershop.com
Career Zone/Spherion	www1.joboptions.com
Classifieds 2000	wwwclassifieds2000.com
Cool Jobs	www.cooljobs.com
Global Employer's Network Inc.	www.geni-jobnet.com
Go Jobs Internet Recruiting	www.gojobs.com
Hot Jobs.com	www.hotjobs.yahoo.com
InstaMatch Resume Database	www.instamatch.com
Job Bank	www.jobbank.com
Job Find.com	www.jobfind.com
Job Smart	www.jobsmart.org
Jobs	www.Jobs.com
JobWeb	www.jobweb.com
Monster Board	www.monster.com
Monster Trak	www.monstertrak.com
Net-Temps	www.net-temps.com
Newspaper Classifieds	www.newspapers.com
Recruiters Online Network	www.recruitersonline.com

Resume Archive	www.resumearchive.com
Resunet	www.resunet.com
The Riley Guide	www.rileyguide.com
TrueCareers	www.truecareers.com
U.S. Career Resource Center	www.uscareers.com
U.S. Resume	www.usresume.com
Vault	www.vault.com
Wall Street Journal Ads	www.careers.wsj.com

Military Related Websites

Army Career and Alumni	www.acap.army.mil
Army Transcript Service	www-leav.army.mil/aarts
Corporate Gray Online	www.greentogray.com
Credentialing Opportunities On-Line	www.cool.army.mil
Department of Defense Transition	www.dodtransportal.org
Department of Veteran's Affairs	www.va.gov
Destiny Group	www.destinygroup.com
DoD Dictionary of Military Terms	www.dtic.mil/doctrine/jel/doddict
GI Bill	www.gibill.va.gov
Military Spouse Resource Center	http://milspouse.org
Small Business Administration (SBA)	www.sba.gov
SmartStart for New Vets	www.smartstartvets.org
Standardized Topic Exchange Service (SITES)	www.dmdc.osd.mil/sites
Transition Assistance Online	www.taonline.com
Troops to Teachers	www.proudtoserveagain.com
UMET (Use Your Military Experience and Training)	www.umet-vets.dol.gov
VetJobs	www.vetjobs.com
Workforce Transition Program	www. cwanett.org/military.asp

Salary Research

Salary and Benefits Survey Reports	www.abbott-langer.com
Wages, Earnings, and Benefits	http://stats.bls.gov salary.cgi
Economic Research Institute	www.erieri.com/
Realtor	www.homefair.com
JobStar Salary Surveys	jobsmart.org/tools/salary
Salary.com	www.salary.com

U.S. BLS Occupational
Outlook Handbook   www.bls.gov/oco
Wage Web   www.wageweb.com
Wall Street Journal   www.careerjournal.com/
                                salaries/index.html

Search Engines

Aeiwi   www.aeiwi.com
AOL NetFind   www.aol.com/netfind/
Ask Jeeves!   www.askjeeves.com
Cozy Cabin   www.cozycabin.com
Direct Hit   www.directhit.com
Dmoz   www.dmoz.org
Excite   www.excite.com
Fathead   www.fathead.net/search
Google   www.google.com
HotBot   www.hotbot.com
Info Tiger   www.infotiger.com
Jayde   www.jayde.com
Librarian's Index   http:// lii.org/search
LookSmart   www.looksmart.com
Lycos   www.lycos.com
National Directory   www.national
                                directory.com

NBCi   www.nbci.com
Northern Light   www.northernlight.com
One Key   www.onekey.com
Overture   www.overture.com
QuestFinder   www.questfinder.com
Scrub the Web   www.scrubtheweb.com
Search King   www.searchking.com
SearchPort   www.searchport.org
WebCrawler   www.webcrawler.com

Index

A
Abbreviations, 61
Accomplishments, 8
Applications, 65-68
Assessment tools, 25
Attitude, 4

B
Benefits, 130
Blaming others, 5

C
Career history, 8
Career management, 134-143
Chamber of Commerce, 33
Classified ads, 60
Clubs, 32-33
College career services, 33
Communication skills, 56-59

D
Defense contracting, 44
Department of Defense, 3, 29-30
Department of Labor, 33
Details, 34
Dress, 118

E
Education, 18
Email, 105

Employers:
  needs of, 22-25
Employment:
  agencies, 33
  federal, 40-42
  options, 39-49
Employment readiness programs, 31
Evaluation, 34
Experience, 8

F
Family member preference, 43
Family services and support centers, 30-31
Family support groups, 32
Federal employment, 40-42
Financial aid, 19
Focus, 4, 135
Follow-up, 69, 121
Functional skills (see Transferable skills)

G
Goals, 34

H
Hiring practices, 4

I

International jobs, 48
Internet, 58-59
Interview:
  purposes, 107
  questions, 111-115
Interviews, 106-121

J

Job:
  fairs, 61-64
  fit, 25
  offer, 123-124
  perfect, 25
  satisfaction, 3
  search, 4-6

Job search:
  blues, 37-38
  focus, 4-6
  Internet, 58-59
  plan, 4-5, 28
  power tools, 50-69
  resources, 29-34
  successful, 26
  traditional, 60-64

K

Keywords, 79-80

L

Language, 79-80
Letters:
  cover, 94-100
  job search, 93-105
  resume, 103
  thank you, 100

M

Military exchange system, 45
Military spouse preference,

42-43
Military spouses, 1-2
Mobility, 39
Money:
  educational, 18-19
  finding, 18-19
Motivation, 6

N

Networking, 6, 50-52
Newspapers, 34
Non-appropriated fund positions, 43-44

O

Objective, 19-22, 28-29
Office of Personnel
  Management, 40
Officers' spouses, 3
One-Stop Career Centers, 19
Opportunities, 2
Organizers, 35-37

P

Planning, 27-28
Private industry, 47-48
Professional associations, 32-33

Q

Questions:
  answer, 109-116
  ask, 117-118
  illegal, 116

R

References, 53-55
Relocation, 3
Resources, 29
Responsibility, 5
Resumes, 70-92
Retention rates, 3

S
Salary:
  history, 66, 129
  negotiations, 125-129
  requirements, 66
Sales sound bite, 56-57
Self-employment, 45-47
Selling, 7
Skills:
  self-management, 13-15
  transferable, 15-17
  updating, 18
  work content, 17-18
Strengths, 5
Success:
  achieving, 38
  defining, 6

T
Telephone, 57-58
Time management, 37
Tracking, 34-36
Transferable skills, 15-17
Transition assistance programs, 31-32

V
Volunteer experiences, 8
Volunteering, 48

W
Women, 2
Work:
  content skills, 17-18
  experience, 8
  locations, 131
  schedules, 131

The Author

JANET I. FARLEY, Ed.M., writes from both a personal and professional point of view. On the personal side, she is an Army wife and a Marine Corps brat, and is the mother of two daughters. On the professional side, she is a highly experienced career counselor and military transition specialist who has worked in the field of spousal employment for nearly 10 years. She has worked extensively with the military's transition program across the globe from Fort Huachuca, Arizona to Fort Gordon, Georgia to Mannheim, Heidelberg, and Stuttgart, Germany.

Janet earned her Master's Degree in Human Services and Human Resource Education from Boston University and her Bachelor of Science Degree in Business and Management from the University of Maryland. She is considered a subject matter expert in the field of job search, and her advice articles have appeared in numerous career-related publications such as *Succeed: The Magazine for Continuing Education and Career Development, Wall Street Journal,* and *Times Publishing.*

Janet currently resides with her military spouse in Stuttgart, Germany, where she is a freelance writer, an instructor, and a private career consultant. She can be contacted via email at janetfarley@hotmail.com.

Career Resources

THE FOLLOWING CAREER RESOURCES are available directly from Impact Publications. Full descriptions of each title as well as nine downloadable catalogs, videos, and software can be found on our website: www.impactpublications.com. Complete the following form or list the titles, include shipping (see formula at the end), enclose payment, and send your order to:

IMPACT PUBLICATIONS
9104 Manassas Drive, Suite N
Manassas Park, VA 20111-5211 USA
1-800-361-1055 (orders only)
Tel. 703-361-7300 or Fax 703-335-9486
Email: info@impactpublications.com
Quick & easy online ordering: www.impactpublications.com

Orders from individuals must be prepaid by check, money order, or major credit card. We accept telephone, fax, and email orders.

Qty.	TITLES	Price	TOTAL
Featured Title			
_____	Jobs and the Military Spouse	$17.95	_____
Changing Addictive and Not-So-Hot Behaviors			
_____	Denial Is Not a River in Egypt	11.95	_____
_____	Failing Forward	19.99	_____
_____	No One Is Unemployable	29.95	_____
_____	No One Will Hire Me!	13.95	_____
_____	Passages Through Recovery	14.00	_____
_____	Recovery Book	15.95	_____
_____	Sex, Drugs, Gambling and Chocolate	15.95	_____
_____	Stop the Chaos	12.95	_____
_____	Top Ten Dumb Career Mistakes	14.95	_____
_____	The Truth About Addiction and Recovery	14.00	_____
_____	Understanding the Twelve Steps	12.00	_____
_____	You Can Heal Your Life	17.95	_____

Attitude and Motivation

____ 100 Ways to Motivate Yourself	18.99	____
____ Change Your Attitude	15.99	____
____ Reinventing Yourself	18.99	____

Inspiration and Empowerment

____ 101 Secrets of Highly Effective Speakers	15.95	____
____ Do What You Love for the Rest of Your Life	24.95	____
____ Do What You Love, the Money Will Follow	13.95	____
____ Doing Work You Love	14.95	____
____ Eat That Frog!	19.95	____
____ Focal Point	21.95	____
____ If Life Is a Game, These Are the Rules	15.00	____
____ If Success Is a Game, These Are the Rules	17.50	____
____ Life Strategies	21.95	____
____ Power of Purpose	20.00	____
____ Practical Dreamer's Handbook	13.95	____
____ Right Words at the Right Time	25.00	____
____ Self Matters	13.95	____
____ Seven Habits of Highly Effective People	14.00	____
____ Who Moved My Cheese?	19.95	____

Testing and Assessment

____ Career Interests to Job Chart	19.95	____
____ Career Tests	12.95	____
____ Discover the Best Jobs for You	15.95	____
____ Discover What You're Best At	14.00	____
____ Do What You Are	18.95	____
____ Finding Your Perfect Work	16.95	____
____ Gifts Differing	16.95	____
____ I Could Do Anything If Only I Knew What It Was	13.95	____
____ I Don't Know What I Want, But I Know It's Not This	14.00	____
____ I'm Not Crazy, I'm Just Not You	16.95	____
____ Making Vocational Choices	34.95	____
____ Now, Discover Your Strengths	26.00	____
____ Pathfinder	14.00	____
____ Please Understand Me II	15.95	____
____ What Should I Do With My Life?	24.95	____
____ What Type Am I?	14.95	____
____ What's Your Type of Career?	17.95	____

Career Exploration and Job Strategies

____ 25 Jobs That Have It All	12.95	____
____ 50 Cutting Edge Jobs	15.95	____
____ 100 Great Jobs and How to Get Them	17.95	____
____ 101 Ways to Recession-Proof Your Career	14.95	____
____ Adams Jobs Almanac	16.95	____
____ American Almanac of Jobs and Salaries	20.00	____

____	America's 100 Top Jobs for People Without a Four-Year Degree	19.95	____
____	America's Top Jobs for People Without a Four-Year Degree	16.95	____
____	Back Door Guide to Short-Term Job Opportunities	21.95	____
____	Best Jobs for the 21st Century	19.95	____
____	Break the Rules	15.00	____
____	Career Change	14.95	____
____	Career Intelligence	15.95	____
____	Change Your Job, Change Your Life	17.95	____
____	Complete Guide to Occupational Exploration	39.95	____
____	Complete Idiot's Guide to Changing Careers	17.95	____
____	Cool Careers for Dummies	19.99	____
____	Dancing Naked	17.95	____
____	Directory of Executive Recruiters	49.95	____
____	Don't Send a Resume	16.95	____
____	Enhanced Guide for Occupational Exploration	34.95	____
____	Enhanced Occupational Outlook Handbook	37.95	____
____	Five Secrets to Finding a Job	12.95	____
____	Help! Was That a Career Limiting Move?	10.95	____
____	High-Tech Careers for Low-Tech People	14.95	____
____	How to Be a Permanent Temp	12.95	____
____	How to Get a Job and Keep It	16.95	____
____	How to Succeed Without a Career Path	13.95	____
____	Job Hunting Guide	14.95	____
____	Job Smarts	16.95	____
____	Knock 'Em Dead	12.95	____
____	Me, Myself, and I, Inc.	17.95	____
____	No One Is Unemployable	29.95	____
____	Occupational Outlook Handbook	16.95	____
____	O*NET Dictionary of Occupational Titles	39.95	____
____	Quit Your Job and Grow Some Hair	15.95	____
____	Rites of Passage at $100,000 to $1 Million+	29.95	____
____	Switching Careers	17.95	____
____	What Color Is Your Parachute?	17.95	____
____	Who's Running Your Career	14.95	____

Internet Job Search

____	100 Top Internet Job Sites	12.95	____
____	Adams Internet Job Search Almanac	10.95	____
____	America's Top Internet Job Sites	19.95	____
____	CareerXroads (annual)	26.95	____
____	Career Exploration On the Internet	24.95	____
____	Cyberspace Job Search Kit	18.95	____
____	Directory of Websites for International Jobs	19.95	____
____	e-Resumes	11.95	____
____	Electronic Resumes and Online Networking	13.99	____
____	Everything Online Job Search Book	12.95	____
____	Guide to Internet Job Searching	14.95	____

_____ Haldane's Best Employment Websites
       for Professionals   15.95   _____
_____ Job-Hunting On the Internet   9.95   _____
_____ Job Search Online for Dummies (w/CD-ROM)   24.99   _____

Resumes and Letters

_____ 101 Best .Com Resumes and Letters   11.95   _____
_____ 101 Best Cover Letters   11.95   _____
_____ 101 Best Resumes   10.95   _____
_____ 101 Great Resumes   9.99   _____
_____ 101 More Best Resumes   11.95   _____
_____ 101 Great Tips for a Dynamite Resume   13.95   _____
_____ 175 Best Cover Letters   14.95   _____
_____ 201 Dynamite Job Search Letters   19.95   _____
_____ 201 Killer Cover Letters   16.95   _____
_____ $100,000 Resumes   16.95   _____
_____ Adams Resume Almanac, with Disk   19.95   _____
_____ America's Top Resumes for
      America's Top Jobs   19.95   _____
_____ Asher's Bible of Executive Resumes   29.95   _____
_____ Best KeyWords for Resumes,
      Cover Letters, and Interviews   17.95   _____
_____ Best Resumes and CVs for International Jobs 24.95   _____
_____ Best Resumes for $100,000+ Jobs   24.95   _____
_____ Best Resumes for $75,000+ Executive Jobs   15.95   _____
_____ Best Resumes for People Without
      a Four-Year Degree   19.95   _____
_____ Best Cover Letters for $100,000+ Jobs   24.95   _____
_____ Building a Great Resume   15.00   _____
_____ Building Your Career Portfolio   13.99   _____
_____ Cover Letter Magic   16.95   _____
_____ Cover Letters for Dummies   16.99   _____
_____ Cover Letters That Knock 'Em Dead   12.95   _____
_____ Cyberspace Resume Kit   18.95   _____
_____ Dynamite Cover Letters   14.95   _____
_____ Dynamite Resumes   14.95   _____
_____ e-Resumes   14.95   _____
_____ Electronic Resumes and Online Networking   13.99   _____
_____ The Everything Cover Letter Book   12.95   _____
_____ The Everything Resume Book   12.95   _____
_____ Expert Resumes for Computer and Web Jobs   16.95   _____
_____ Federal Resume Guidebook   21.95   _____
_____ Gallery of Best Cover Letters   18.95   _____
_____ Gallery of Best Resumes   18.95   _____
_____ Gallery of Best Resumes for 2-Year Degree 16.95   _____

Graduates   18.95   _____
_____ Global Resume and CV Guide   17.95   _____
_____ Haldane's Best Cover Letters for Professionals 15.95 _____

_____	Haldane's Best Resumes for Professionals	15.95 _____
_____	High Impact Resumes and Letters	19.95 _____
_____	Internet Resumes	14.95 _____
_____	Military Resumes and Cover Letters	19.95 _____
_____	Overnight Resume	12.95 _____
_____	Power Resumes	12.95 _____
_____	Professional Resumes for Executives, Managers, & Other Administrators	19.95 _____
_____	Professional Resumes for Accounting, Tax, Finance, and Law	19.95 _____
_____	Proven Resumes	19.95 _____
_____	Resume Catalog	15.95 _____
_____	Resume Magic	18.95 _____
_____	Resume Shortcuts	14.95 _____
_____	Resumes for Dummies	16.99 _____
_____	Resumes for the Health Care Professional	14.95 _____
_____	Resumes in Cyberspace	14.95 _____
_____	Resumes That Knock 'Em Dead	12.95 _____
_____	The Savvy Resume Writer	12.95 _____
_____	Sure-Hire Resumes	14.95 _____

Networking

_____	Connecting With Success	20.95 _____
_____	Dynamite Telesearch	12.95 _____
_____	A Foot in the Door	14.95 _____
_____	Golden Rule of Schmoozing	12.95 _____
_____	Great Connections	11.95 _____
_____	How to Work a Room	14.00 _____
_____	Masters of Networking	16.95 _____
_____	Networking Smart	22.95 _____
_____	Power Networking	14.95 _____
_____	Power Schmoozing	12.95 _____
_____	The Savvy Networker	13.95 _____

Dress, Image, and Etiquette

_____	Dressing Smart for Men	16.95 _____
_____	Dressing Smart for Women	16.95 _____
_____	First Five Minutes	14.95 _____
_____	New Professional Image	12.95 _____
_____	New Women's Dress for Success	13.99 _____
_____	Power Etiquette	14.95 _____
_____	Professional Impressions	14.95 _____

Interviews

_____	101 Dynamite Questions to Ask At Your Job Interview	13.95 _____
_____	Behavior-Based Interviewing	12.95 _____
_____	Great Interview	12.95 _____
_____	Haldane's Best Answers to Tough Interview Questions	15.95 _____

____ Interview for Success	15.95	_____
____ Interview Rehearsal Book	12.00	_____
____ Job Interviews for Dummies	16.99	_____
____ Nail the Job Interview!	13.95	_____
____ The Savvy Interviewer	10.95	_____
____ Sweaty Palms	11.95	_____
____ Winning Interviews for $100,000+ Jobs	17.95	_____

Salary Negotiations

____ Better Than Money	18.95	_____
____ Dynamite Salary Negotiations	15.95	_____
____ Get a Raise in 7 Days	14.95	_____
____ Get More Money On Your Next Job	17.95	_____
____ Get Paid More and Promoted Faster	19.95	_____
____ Haldane's Best Salary Tips for Professionals	15.95	_____

Government and Nonprofit Jobs

____ Complete Guide to Public Employment	19.95	_____
____ Directory of Federal Jobs and Employers	21.95	_____
____ Federal Applications That Get Results	23.95	_____
____ Federal Employment From A to Z	14.50	_____
____ Federal Jobs in Law Enforcement	14.95	_____
____ FBI Careers	18.95	_____
____ Find a Federal Job Fast!	15.95	_____
____ Jobs and Careers With Nonprofit Organizations	17.95	_____
____ Ten Steps to a Federal Job	39.95	_____

International and Travel Jobs

____ Back Door Guide to Short-Term Job Adventures	21.95	_____
____ Careers in International Affairs	17.95	_____
____ Careers in Travel, Tourism, and Hospitality	19.95	_____
____ Career Opportunities in Travel and Tourism	18.95	_____
____ Directory of Websites for International Jobs	19.95	_____
____ Flight Attendant Job Finder and Career Guide	16.95	_____
____ Global Resume and CV Guide	17.95	_____
____ Inside Secrets to Finding a Career in Travel	14.95	_____
____ International Jobs	19.00	_____
____ International Job Finder	19.95	_____
____ Jobs for Travel Lovers	19.95	_____
____ Teaching English Abroad	15.95	_____
____ Work Abroad	15.95	_____
____ Work Your Way Around the World	17.95	_____

SUBTOTAL   _____

SUBTOTAL   _____

Virginia residents add 4.5 % sales tax   .... _____

POSTAGE/HANDLING ($5 for first
                product and 8% of SUBTOTAL).................... _____

TOTAL ENCLOSED --------------------┐

SHIP TO:

NAME   _____

ADDRESS_____

          _____

          _____

          _____

PAYMENT METHOD:

❑   I enclose check/money order for $ _____ made payable to
     IMPACT PUBLICATIONS.

❑   Please charge $_____ to my credit card:

❑   Visa   ❑   MasterCard   ❑   American Express   ❑   Discover

Card # _____   Expiration date: _____/_____

Signature _____

Toll Free: 1-800-361-1055
Fax 703-335-9486

Keep in Touch . . .
On the Web!

www.impactpublications.com
www.ishoparoundtheworld.com
www.hoteltravelshop.com
www.mycruiseshop.com
www.contentfortravel.com
www.winningthejob.com
www.veteransworld.com
www.contentforcareers.com